T0277746

FROM THE FILMS OF

Harry Potter

THE OFFICIAL
HOGWARTS BOOK
OF CROSS-STITCH

FROM THE FILMS OF

Harry Potter

THE OFFICIAL
HOGWARTS BOOK
OF CROSS-STITCH

PATTERNS BY WILLOW POLSON

WRITTEN BY JODY REVENSON

INSIGHT
EDITIONS

SAN RAFAEL · LOS ANGELES · LONDON

✕✕✕✕ CONTENTS ✕✕✕✕

✕✕✕✕ INTRODUCTION ✕✕✕✕

It is a wonderful thing to come upon a place you never knew existed before or have an experience that changes your point of view. This happened to Harry Potter in *Harry Potter and the Sorcerer's Stone* when he was taken to Diagon Alley by Rubeus Hagrid. After a brick wall behind The Leaky Cauldron in London folds in upon itself, opening a new doorway, Harry is introduced to the wizarding world. A world of flying brooms, wand shops, and a school that teaches spells, charms, and potions. In short, he experiences magic.

Creation is also magic. By taking raw materials and working with focus, skill, and experience, you manifest something with your own two hands that never existed before. With the skills learned and projects realized in *Harry Potter: The Official Hogwarts Book of Cross-Stitch*, you can work your own creative magic. As you enjoy the sight, sound, and feel of drawing colored threads through fabric to create a picture, know that you're experiencing what people around the world have enjoyed for generations. Although stitching on fabric has been around for many millennia, cross-stitch as the primary stitch used in a pattern has been around roughly as long as Hogwarts School of Witchcraft and Wizardry in the Harry Potter films.

This book is intended as a stepping stone into the fascinating world of cross-stitch. It explains exactly what a beginner needs to know, with detailed instructions on the stitches, equipment, and techniques needed to complete a wide variety of projects. Within these pages, you'll find opportunities to create practical objects for daily use, like a caddy in the shape of a Bertie Bott's Every Flavour Beans box (pg 131) that can hold your quills and pens. You'll also find patterns for bookmarks, to keep your place while rereading your favorite books about a boy wizard.

They are meant to offer a range so you can get as elaborate and challenging as you'd like. The journey into the world of needle arts is yours to explore in the ways that make you happiest.

CROSS-STITCH: THE BASICS

Cross-stitch is as easy as the swish-and-flick wand movement taught by Professor Flitwick in the Harry Potter films! Once you get the technique down, it will feel like second nature. So, like the list of school supplies that accompanies the first years' acceptance letter to Hogwarts, here's what you'll need to get started.

Fortunately, you won't have to empty a vault at Gringotts Wizarding Bank to begin cross-stitching. A hoop, some floss (thread), fabric, and a needle are all you need. You can get super fancy and buy all kinds of accessories, but don't feel you have to—a pair of regular scissors will cut floss just as well as a pair of little embroidery scissors. So, let's talk basics.

FABRIC

Cross-stitch can be done on most kinds of fabric (though we imagine using Harry's Invisibility Cloak from the films would be tricky), but the majority of the projects in this book use Aida cloth. Aida is a cloth made specifically for cross-stitch, and it is woven in such a way that it looks like a grid with holes at even intervals, so you know exactly where your needle should go. Aida cloth comes in a large variety of colors, so you don't always have to use white. Aida also comes in precut sizes as well as rolls that you can cut to your ideal specifications—if you're planning to do more than one piece, your best bet may be to buy the roll.

Aida cloth comes in different counts—the count refers to the number of holes per inch of fabric. The higher the count, the tighter the stitches will be, and the smaller the final piece will be. The easiest to use is 14-count Aida (14 stitches to the inch).

Occasionally, projects in this book call for evenweave linen or perforated plastic instead. Perforated plastic has holes much like Aida cloth and, for either of those fabrics, we'll be using the 14-count option. For each pattern in this book, we'll let you know the fabric we're using and, if it's Aida cloth or perforated plastic, we'll remind you of the count.

FLOSS

Cross-stitch is done with cotton embroidery floss, which is made up of six thin strands twisted together. There are several brands, but for this book we are using DMC floss, which is one of the most common and accessible brands. The color names for floss, even DMC floss, tend to change. But DMC also uses numbers to identify specific hues. In the charts for each pattern, you'll see both color names and numbers provided. If the names don't match, trust the numbers!

Many of the patterns in this book require three strands of floss, but in general, the cloth count determines how many of the six strands you will use.

11-count: 3–4 strands
12-count: 3 strands
14-count: 3 strands
16-count: 2–3 strands
18-count: 2 strands
20-count: 1–2 strands
24-count or higher: 1 strand

If you prefer a denser look to your finished work (so that the Xs that make up a cross-stitch stitch look more like full blocks of color), use three strands of floss on

14-count. We generally don't recommend going any higher, though—your piece will start to look clunky, and stitching will be difficult.

These projects may have a tendency toward flash and flare, like the former Defense Against the Dark Arts professor, Gilderoy Lockhart. So you'll find that a few patterns call for gold metallic thread from the DMC Pearl Cotton Metallic line. With this special floss, you'll find two larger strands made up of several very small ones. When using this specialty thread, separate the two larger strands as described on page 10. Each of these is considered one strand in the patterns given here. Do not separate the threads any further. You may also want to use a needle threader as the ends of the two larger strands tend to fray easily. Use short lengths of this thread, about 12 inches or so, because the metallic coating will separate from the inner core over time as it's drawn repeatedly through the fabric.

NEEDLE

Because Aida cloth already has holes in it, the best needle to use is a tapestry needle. It has a blunt tip that will pass through the material as easily as Hermione did when she relaxed after she, Harry, and Ron got caught in Devil's Snare. Tapestry needles come in a variety of sizes, and you'll want to make sure you don't use too large a size—a too-big needle will stretch the holes in your cloth and distort your project. For 14-count Aida, we recommend using a size 24 tapestry needle. If a pattern does require a smaller needle for detailed work, a sharp sewing needle, size 12, is ideal.

HOOP

Just like a wand is to a witch or a wizard, a hoop is the cross-stitcher's best resource: A hoop will keep the fabric tight and your stitches neat and uniform. People have their preferences when it comes to the size of hoop to use: Some prefer to work the pattern in sections, using smaller hoops that are easier to hold in your hand; others prefer to have the entire pattern visible in the hoop. The choice is yours. There are also several kinds of frames to choose from—plastic, wood, screw frame, and snap frame—but the most common and easiest hoops to find are plastic and wood. Plastic tends to hold the fabric better, but the wood frame can transition easily from working hoop to display hoop.

Some stitchers prefer to use a scroll frame or stretcher bars with tacks when working on larger pieces. This way, they won't have to move a hoop around from section to section, which can cause rings in the fabric that may need to be ironed out. For the purposes of the patterns in this book, your hoop should be large enough to encompass the whole piece at once.

SCISSORS

Any scissors will do when you're creating a cross-stitch project, in much the same way talented flyer Harry Potter can soar on an enchanted broom, whether it's a scraggly one from his first flying class or on his Firebolt. However, a pair of small embroidery scissors does have one distinct advantage—their small, sharp points come in handy if you need to remove stitches.

Before you stitch your own Hogwarts crest or portrait of Hagrid's hut, there are a few things you need to set up your cloth and thread.

CUTTING THE CLOTH

Just as Ron Weasley in *Harry Potter and the Sorcerer's Stone* mispronounced the levitation spell *Wingardium Leviosa*, mistakes can happen in cross-stitch, such as miscounting stitches or running out of thread, and all of them can be fixed except one: running out of fabric. There is no coming back from cutting your fabric too small and running out of room for the pattern. It's always best to leave yourself a healthy border of at least 3 to 4 inches (7.5 to 10 cm) on each side. So, if your finished piece is 4 x 6 inches (10 x 12 cm), your piece of fabric should be at least 7 x 9 inches (18 x 23 cm). This may seem like a lot, but it's better to have excess than to run out. It will also help when it comes time to mount your piece. Each pattern in this book gives you the size cloth you need, including a healthy border.

WHERE DO I START TO STITCH?

It's always best to start stitching in the middle of a pattern; if you start in a corner and misjudge the placement, you could run out of fabric! So, it's important to find the middle of your piece of cloth, which is easier than incanting a location spell: Just fold the fabric in half lengthwise, then in half widthwise, and where the two creases intersect is your center. Insert your needle, or even a pin, into this intersection so you won't lose your place when you pull the fabric taut in your hoop.

A HOOP AND A HOLLER

Hoops have two parts: the inner (smaller) hoop and the outer (larger) hoop. On some hoops, the inner has a little lip that you can feel, which helps the fabric stay in place. If yours has that lip, that lip faces up. Place the inner hoop on a flat surface, then lay the fabric on top (the lip should now be against the fabric). Center the fabric using the marked center as a guide. The outer hoop has a screw and nut at the top; unscrew it as far as you want without the nut falling off, then carefully place it on top of the fabric. Push it down until the two hoops meet and the fabric is taut. Tighten the screw just enough to hold the fabric, then pull the edges of the fabric to make it as tight as you want. Some people like a little give, others like it as tight as a drum—it's up to you. Once the fabric is taut, tighten the screw until it feels completely secure.

NEEDLE AND THREAD

Before threading the needle, you need to get the floss ready. Aim to cut a piece of floss about 18 to 24 inches long. If you're using a length of floss that's too long, you'll risk it tangling and knotting while you stitch. Then tap the end of the floss until the individual strands separate (if one end won't do it, try the other). Hold on to the bundle with the fingertips of one hand and slide a single strand out the end with your other hand. Set this aside and repeat twice more. Once you have three loose strands, gather them together and thread them, as one, through the eye of your needle. You're ready to go!

DON'T GET YOUR WAND—OR FLOSS—IN A KNOT

There are some cross-stitchers who say you should never knot your floss, and there are some good reasons for not knotting. The decision comes down to how much you care about the back of your piece. Some insist that the back has to look as pristine as the front. But don't let the back of your piece stress you out like Ron at Quidditch tryouts! If you're a beginner and you're not worried about the look of the back, go ahead and knot your floss. Just simply tie a small knot at the end of your thread.

If you're planning to display your piece in a frame, however, it's best not to use knots, as they will leave lumps when mounted on the frame board. If you're displaying the piece in a hoop, you won't have to mount the piece on board, and knots will work just fine.

NOT KNOTTING

If you want to go no-knot, when you pull your thread through the first hole, hold about 1 inch (2.5 cm) of thread on the back side with your finger. Keep holding it while you stitch the next few stitches over that thread. This is called anchoring the thread.

NOT IN THE BACK

Whether you use a knot or an anchor, when you are finished with that thread, turn your piece over and work your needle under a couple stitches, pull the thread through, and cut.

THE KNOTLESS LOOP

This is a neat and super-easy way to avoid a knot, if you're using two strands of floss. Cut a piece of floss twice the length you need, then only pull out a single strand instead of two. Bring the two ends of the single strand together, so you have a loop at the other end. Thread the side with the ends through the needle. Come up through the fabric for your first stitch, leaving the loop in back, then come back down and thread the needle through the loop. Gently pull until the loop flattens at the back.

WASTE KNOTS

For this technique, knot your thread and, coming up from the back, go through the top of the cloth 4 to 6 inches from where you're actually going to start stitching. Then, when you've stitched enough of your piece that the floss feels secure, cut off the knot above the fabric. Quickly thread your needle at the back of your pattern, then bring the floss through your stitches from the back. Technically, you're wasting some of your floss, but you'll be able to anchor your piece when you need to, and get the knot out of your way quickly to avoid pulling it through your grid or blocking the area you want to stitch into.

READING PATTERNS

Cross-stitch is just what it sounds like—it's just making a series of Xs, which are made up of two small stitches that cross diagonally. But before we get to the stitches, like learning to read tea leaves as Professor Trelawney taught her Divination class in *Harry Potter and the Prisoner of Azkaban*, let's learn how to read a pattern.

HOW TO READ A PATTERN

The patterns in this book are rendered in what is called counted cross-stitch. It is called that because you literally count the number of colored blocks on the pattern and stitch that number. To some it may sound tedious or intimidating, but it's actually much easier than working on a printed pattern. Sometimes the printing isn't done well, or the pattern is printed crooked on the fabric, which makes reading it a disaster. In counted cross-stitch there is no guessing—if you have five red blocks, you make five red stitches.

A cross-stitch pattern is made up of colored blocks on a grid (just like the grid of your cloth). Each block on the grid represents one X of cross-stitch. The colors correspond to the color chart, which tells you which color floss to use. Some patterns with several colors will also include symbols in the colored blocks to make it even easier to determine which color you should use.

PATTERN PARTICULARS

1. On each pattern, you'll see two red lines—one vertical and one horizontal. These are to help you determine the center of your pattern; where they intersect is the center.

2. The grids on the patterns have darker lines at every ten stitches, to help you with counting larger numbers of stitches.

3. Some of the patterns are spread over two or more pages in order to make the pattern larger and easier to use. To help navigate between pages, a repeat of five rows from the previous page is shown in gray. Do not stitch the grayed-out section; it is only there for reference.

MAPPING OUT YOUR FIRST STITCH

As stated earlier, the absolute best and easiest place to start a cross-stitch project is in the middle, so that the pattern is centered on the canvas. But again, this is personal preference—you can start from any point in the pattern. Count the number of stitches (blocks) from the center of the pattern (the intersection of the red lines) to the point you want to stitch, then count the same number of squares on your fabric, using the center you've marked as the reference.

STITCHING WIZARDRY

To cast a spell, witches and wizards must provide the correct acompanying wand movement. Cross-stitch has its own "movement"—and it's an X. So once you're ready with the fabric and needle, and you know how to read a pattern, it's time to cast a cross-stitch!

COMPLETE CROSS-STITCH

A full stitch is made up of two diagonal stitches, and it couldn't be easier. Here's how you create a complete stitch.

1. Make the first part of your X by bringing your needle from the back to the front through one hole (A). This will be the lower-left corner of your stitch. Pull your thread all the way through and insert your needle through the hole that is diagonally to the right (B), and pull the thread through. You should now have a diagonal stitch (like a forward slash: /)—the first part of your cross.

2. Now bring your needle up through the lower-right corner hole (C), and then down through the upper-left corner hole (D). (It's a back slash: \.)

That's it! You've made one complete stitch.

HALF STITCH

Needless to say, if you have a pattern that includes a half stitch, you only make one of these diagonals.

MULTIPLE CROSS-STITCHES

If you have a number of the same color stitches to do, one option you have is to do all the first diagonals together (/////) and then do all the second diagonals (\\\\\) together. To do this:

1. Come up through the bottom left hole (A), go down into the top right hole (B), come up again in the bottom right hole (C), which is now the beginning of your next diagonal stitch, and then down into the next top right hole (D). Repeat for as many full stitches as you need.

2. When you get to the end of your row, work back across the row to complete the stitches in the other direction.

This technique is also really handy when it comes to large sections of color—and can save lots of miscounting headaches. Stitch just the outline of a large color section with the first diagonal, then go back and fill in. This way, if you do miscount the outline, you're only pulling out a handful of single stitches!

TOP TIPS

- Don't pull your thread through too hard—you'll distort the pattern.

- If your thread becomes twisted, turn the piece over and let the needle and thread dangle; let it untwist itself until it stops spinning.

- If your floss keeps getting knotted, cut it a little shorter. If it's getting hard to pull through the fabric, you can buy floss conditioner to make things go smoother.

- If you get a looped knot stuck in the middle of your thread while stitching, you can use a blunt needle to carefully tease the knot apart. Start at the bottom of the loop and pull gently on the threads until the loop tucks back through itself.

SPECIALTY STITCH: BACKSTITCH

The backstitch, though technically an embroidery stitch, gives you a nice unbroken line that can look pretty against all those Xs. It's just as easy as the cross-stitch:

1. Bring your needle up from back to front (A). Take your needle down into hole to the horizontal right (this is B). This is one stitch.

2. For your second stitch, come up in the hole to the left of A (this is C), then back down into the hole of A. This is the back part of the backstitch.

3. To make the next stitch, come up in the hole to the left of C, then down into C; continue to come up through the hole to the left in the line, and coming down into the hole of the previous stitch. You should now have a straight line!

CARRYING THE THREAD

You've got little bits of green color in different places all over the pattern—do you have to cut the thread and restart for every section?

Not necessarily. If the sections are in close proximity, you can do what is called "carrying the thread." This just means not cutting the thread between the sections. You only want to do this over two or three blank squares, at most—any more than that and the carried thread can start showing through the holes in the fabric. If you're carrying across an area that's already stitched, you can go a little farther, but just weave your needle under the stitched section, to tack down that carried thread.

MISCOUNTS

Miscounting stitches happens to everyone, no matter how experienced you are. It's just a fact of cross-stitch life! There is nothing worse than getting halfway through a pattern and realizing that two sections aren't matching up. So, stop occasionally and just do a quick check to make sure everything is lining up on the fabric as it is in the pattern. Better to find out sooner rather than later!

Don't freak out if you've miscounted—the mistake is easily fixable. Just take your needle and pick out the wayward stitches. If it's a section that's already been completed, use a seam ripper or the tip of your embroidery scissors to clip out a few stitches—always working from the back—and then pick out the rest with your needle.

But, most important, there's nothing to get upset about. It's all part of the process!

CLEANING

Cleaning your fabric can start as early as before your first stitch, when you may want to test the cloth for colorfastness. A drop of baby shampoo or unscented soap can make an excellent gentle detergent. And no matter how careful you are, your project may get soiled along the way. No worries here, though—you can wash your piece even after you've finished stitching. Just place it in a bowl of tepid water mixed with a mild laundry detergent or baby shampoo, swish it around (don't rub or twist the fabric), and let it set. Then rinse (don't wring it out), lay it flat on a bath towel, and roll up the towel to squeeze out the excess water. Lay flat to dry. Washing your piece is also great for getting out the circles that your hoop leaves in the cloth.

DISPLAY (OF COURSE)

Like the paintings on the walls of Hogwarts halls, once your piece is finished, you'll want to frame it and display it. There are lots of ways you can do it, all of which are pretty easy. But first, you have to get the piece ready for framing.

PREPPING YOUR PIECE

Before you frame, you might want to wash your fabric (see page 14). Whether you wash the fabric or not, you're definitely going to need to iron it. Put a clean, white dish towel down on your ironing board. Lay the piece facedown and place another dish towel on top. With your iron set on steam, slowly press the piece until the creases are gone. If your iron has a "Wool" heat setting, that's what we'd recommend. Avoid going any higher, especially if you're using metallic or non-cotton threads.

HOOPING YOUR PIECE

For this, you'll need a nice bamboo or wood hoop and some all-purpose glue. Place your piece in the hoop, making sure the piece is centered and it is nice and taut. Check to see that the screw closure is centered as well, because that is what you are going to use to hang it. Trim the leftover fabric down to about 1 inch (2.5 cm)—you want just enough to fold inside that bottom hoop. Draw a thin line of glue around the inside of the bottom hoop, then press your leftover fabric border into the glue line.

FRAMING YOUR PIECE

There are a lot of ways to frame your work, from professional framing to just taping your piece to a board and putting it in a frame. If you're using a photo frame, the easiest way is to trim your piece, leaving about 1 inch of border. Place it in the frame, insert the back of the frame so the border hangs over the sides, and tack down the border to the back of the frame (or don't—it's the back of the piece, so who's going to see it?).

If you're worried about wrinkles, a great alternative is to use a self-adhesive mounting board. This board has one side with a strong adhesive; just cut it to the size you need (if you're putting it in a frame, use the back of the frame as your guide), peel off the sticky side, and place your piece on it (you can lift it up and rearrange as much as you'd like). Press down to smooth out any wrinkles, then place it in the frame.

ONLINE RESOURCES

Some of the patterns, including the Gryffindor Crest (page 31) and Chocolate Frog 3-D Box (page 127) include optional finishing instructions that differ from the traditional frame method. Additional reference images are free and available at www.insighteditions.com/hogwartscross-stitch. Please refer to this URL whenever you see this symbol ⚡ in the book.

THE ONLY CROSS-STITCH RULE: DO IT YOUR WAY

The beauty of cross-stitch is that there really isn't a wrong way to do it—no wrong way to hold your hoop, work a pattern, or even mount your piece. If you find a way of stitching that works better than how it's described here, go for it! If you want to knot your floss or use a frame rather than a hoop, why not? There are no rules. Do what works for you. Once you start stitching, you'll find your own pace and your own style.

And have fun!

HOGWARTS HOUSE CRESTS

As seen in the films, each house at Hogwarts School of Witchcraft and Wizardry—Gryffindor, Slytherin, Ravenclaw, and Hufflepuff—has its own distinct crest, rendered in the house colors and including the house animal. These crests are seen on the students' individual trunks, on Quidditch fan gear, and most important, on their robes.

The individual house crests, and the all-inclusive Hogwarts crest, were designed by the graphics department. "When we're thinking about a crest or an insignia," graphic designer Miraphora Mina explains, "we're thinking about how we can bring the personality of the person or the institution into the design, and what details will help tell that story." Considering the thousand-year history of the school, Mina researched medieval illustrations for inspiration. She also included the traditional elements of a heraldic crest: a name or motto, a shield with its colors and elements, and a helmet or crown.

These four Hogwarts house crests have been simplified without the house name lettered on them to make stitching easier for first-time stitchers. Each of the four patterns can be finished in one of three ways: framed in a hoop, as demonstrated by the Slytherin and Ravenclaw crests; as a sew-on patch for your clothes, shown in the Hufflepuff crest; or as a piece of jewelry, in the Gryffindor crest. To change this up, apply the pattern for the house in question to the materials suggested for whichever you prefer.

For the films, the graphics department also designed the crests for Beauxbatons Academy of Magic and Durmstrang Institute.

SLYTHERIN CREST

×××××××××××××××××××××××××××××××

Slytherins are known for their pride, ambition, and cunning, which would serve a cross-stitcher well—this craft encourages a steady attention to detail and the motivation to complete each project (and then there's a lot of pride to be had when you finish!).

Harry's nemesis, Draco Malfoy, is a talented wizard who succeeds at many things. But when Draco is recruited by Voldemort in *Harry Potter and the Half-Blood Prince* to kill Albus Dumbledore, he finds this is one assignment he cannot complete. Tom Felton, who plays Draco, considers that "he realizes this is not really the life for him." In *Harry Potter and the Deathly Hallows – Part 1*, though he recognizes Harry's appearance under a Stinging Jinx, he does not confirm his identity to the Death Eaters at Malfoy Manor. "I don't know if he's looking for a stroke of redemption," says Felton. "He just knows deep down he doesn't want to kill Harry. As hard as he would want to be like his dad, he can't."

When cross-stitching this crest, it may be well worth remembering that a Slytherin's ambition to succeed is often a good thing. It's up to you to use that drive to see your patterns through to the end.

PATTERN INFORMATION

- **FABRIC:** 14-count light green Aida, 8 x 9 in
- **NEEDLE SIZE:** 24 tapestry needle
- **STITCH COUNT:** 29 x 37
- **FINISHED SIZE:** 2 x 2.7 in
- **MOUNTING:** 3 or 4 in round hoop
- **DIFFICULTY:** Easy

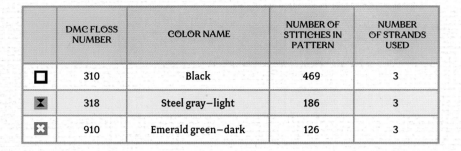

	DMC FLOSS NUMBER	COLOR NAME	NUMBER OF STITICHES IN PATTERN	NUMBER OF STRANDS USED
☐	310	Black	469	3
☒	318	Steel gray—light	186	3
☒	910	Emerald green—dark	126	3

Slytherin Severus Snape turns out to be more of a good person than a bad one due to his affection for Harry's mother, Lily — a fact actor Alan Rickman knew about his character from the start but did not reveal until after the last film premiered.

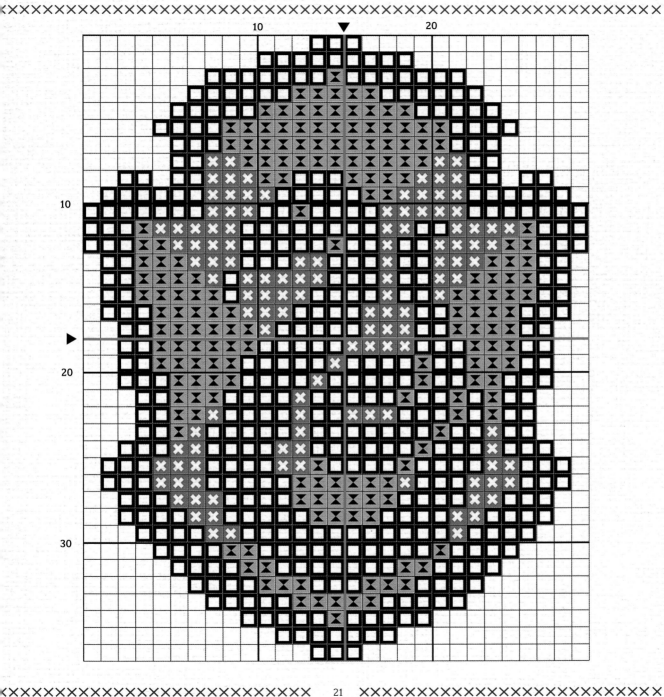

RAVENCLAW CREST

×××××××××××××××××××××××××××××××××××

House founder Rowena Ravenclaw's diadem holds great significance to the Dark Lord Voldemort: it's among the Horcruxes he created, and Harry, Ron, and Hermione are determined to track down and destroy it. Ravenclaw Luna Lovegood calls it the "lost diadem," and when Cho Chang comments in *Harry Potter and the Deathly Hallows – Part 2* that "there isn't a person alive who's seen it," Luna suggests Harry talk to someone who isn't alive: the ghost of Helena Ravenclaw, Rowena's daughter and the ghost of Ravenclaw house known as the Grey Lady.

The Grey Lady was seen in the first two Harry Potter films, dressed in a noblewoman's gown of the late Renaissance. For her appearance in *Deathly Hallows – Part 2*, the now revealed Helena was dressed closer to the tenth-century time period of the founding of Hogwarts, and portrayed by Kelly Macdonald, who wore a simple fitted dress, an embroidered undergown, and a laced-up overgown that featured long draping sleeves.

To rephrase the Ravenclaw motto to apply while working on this pattern, "stitch *within* measure is a stitcher's greatest treasure!"

PATTERN INFORMATION

- **FABRIC:** 14-count white Aida, 8 x 9 in
- **NEEDLE SIZE:** 24 tapestry needle
- **STITCH COUNT:** 29 x 38
- **FINISHED SIZE:** 2 x 2.75 in
- **MOUNTING:** 3 or 4 in round hoop
- **DIFFICULTY:** Easy

	DMC FLOSS NUMBER	COLOR NAME	NUMBER OF STITICHES IN PATTERN	NUMBER OF STRANDS USED
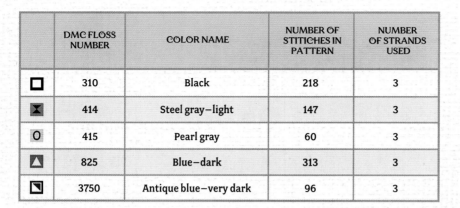	310	Black	218	3
	414	Steel gray—light	147	3
	415	Pearl gray	60	3
	825	Blue—dark	313	3
	3750	Antique blue—very dark	96	3

A fake version of Rowena Ravenclaw's diadem can be seen on a bust in the home of Xenophilius and Luna Lovegood in *Harry Potter and the Deathly Hallows — Part 1.*

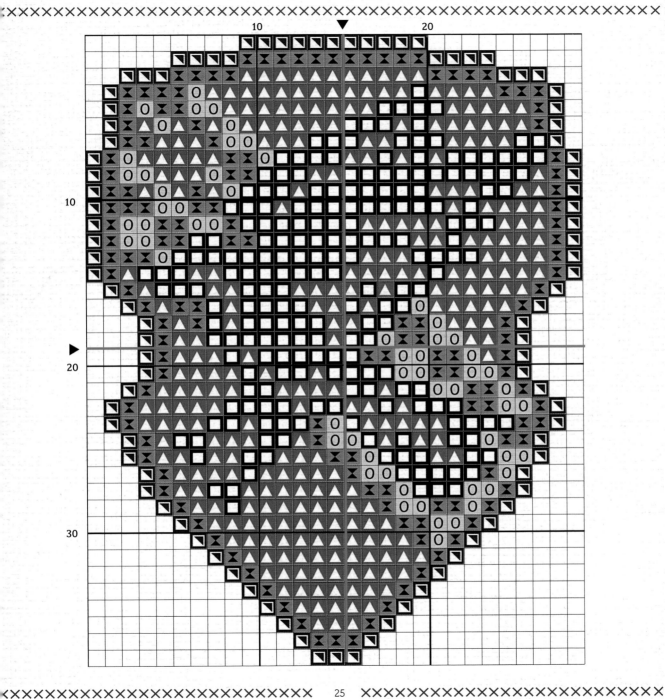

HUFFLEPUFF CREST

×××××××××××××××××××××××××××××××××××

For the Triwizard Tournament that takes place in *Harry Potter and the Goblet of Fire*, the champion chosen by the Goblet to represent Hogwarts is Hufflepuff Cedric Diggory, portrayed by Robert Pattinson. (Harry is also chosen as a fourth champion to everyone's shock.)

Hufflepuffs are known for their dedication, patience, and loyalty. So it's no surprise Pattinson considers his character to be a pretty nice guy. "Cedric is the official competitor in the Tournament," he says. "He's seventeen, in the top year of Hogwarts, and a prefect. He's competitive, but he's got his priorities right. He's honest; he plays fair and sticks to the rules, like he should. But," he admits, "it's actually quite a lot of pressure playing the nice guy! And you know what they say about nice guys . . ."

While working this pattern, remember that patience is a quality shared by both Hufflepuffs and cross-stitchers alike.

PATTERN INFORMATION

- **FABRIC:** 14-count white Aida, 8 x 9 in
- **NEEDLE SIZE:** 24 tapestry needle
- **STITCH COUNT:** 29 x 38
- **FINISHED SIZE:** 2 x 2.75 in
- **MOUNTING:** Sew-on patch
- **DIFFICULTY:** Easy-Intermediate

	DMC FLOSS NUMBER	COLOR NAME	NUMBER OF STITICHES IN PATTERN	NUMBER OF STRANDS USED
☐	310	Black	359	3
☒	414	Steel gray—light	143	3
O	415	Pearl gray	55	3
◪	726	Topaz—light	113	3
N	762	Pearl gray—very light	128	3
♡	White	White	18	3

TOP TIPS:
To make your house crest into a sew-on patch, stitch as usual on 14-count Aida. When the embroidery is finished:

1. Carefully cut around the stitching, leaving a border of one row of fabric.

2. Apply a small amount of craft glue to all the exposed fabric edges, securing them and preventing them from unraveling. Allow this to dry completely.

3. Using six strands of DMC 414 steel gray floss, sew a whip stitch over the edges of the fabric using a similar motion to a single cross-stitch. Bring your needle up through a hole on the edge of the piece, then make a diagonal stitch that goes back down over one hole from where you came up.

4. Continue your whip stitch around the patch until all sides are sealed. Then work your needle under a couple of stitches on the back, pull the thread through, and cut.

5. You can also use a whip stitch to secure the patch to your jacket, book bag, or wizarding robes. For best security, whip your thread through each outside hole, as if you were doing a single cross-stich around the design.

Robert Pattinson learned how to scuba dive for the second task, but said his hardest stunt was repeatedly leaping out of the tree when the Diggorys meet the Weasleys before taking a Portkey to the 422nd Quidditch World Cup.

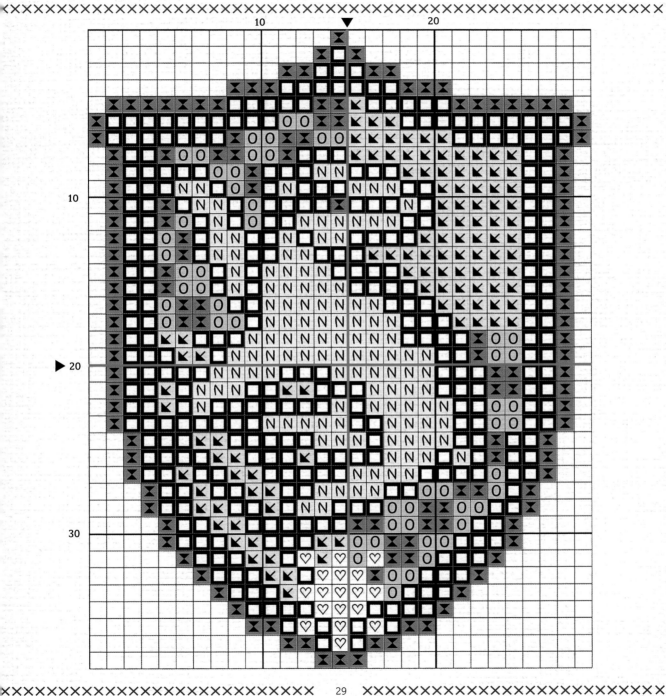

GRYFFINDOR CREST

××××××××××××××××××××××××××××××××××××××

Gryffindor's house colors are red and gold, reflected in the tapestries of their common room and the curtains of their dormitory beds. As production began for *Harry Potter and the Sorcerer's Stone*, production designer Stuart Craig and set decorator Stephenie McMillan wanted the Gryffindor common room to be protective and comfortable, "so we chose those little boxy four-poster beds because they're, in a way, womblike with the red curtains and plain solid posts," said McMillan.

McMillan was challenged in her search for the right material for the bed curtains. She wanted them to be red, of course, and to be printed with magical and astrological symbols in gold. After several weeks of searching antique markets and fabric stores, she finally located the very design she desired. "The design was what I wanted," McMillan said, "but unfortunately, the fabric was purple. Mauve, actually." She told the shopkeeper she liked the pattern but not the color and was about to walk out the door, when the woman asked, "What color would you like it to be?" With that, McMillan was able to drape the bed posts with velvety curtain material the rich scarlet and gold of Gryffindor house.

Gryffindors are known for their courage, bravery, and determination. But remember that you can determine another house for this jewelry pattern if you'd like.

PATTERN INFORMATION

- **FABRIC:** 30-count tan linen, 10 x 12 in
- **NEEDLE SIZE:** 12 sharp sewing needle
- **STITCH COUNT:** 29 x 38
- **FINISHED SIZE:** 1 x 1.25 in
- **MOUNTING:** 2 in circular necklace bezel
- **DIFFICULTY:** Easy-Intermediate

The wall hangings in the Gryffindor common room are digital reproductions of the French fifteenth-century medieval tapestry *The Lady and the Unicorn*, which make ample use of the house colors, red and gold.

	DMC FLOSS NUMBER	COLOR NAME	NUMBER OF STITCHES IN PATTERN	NUMBER OF STRANDS USED
◣	304	Red−medium	89	1
✖	414	Steel gray−dark	108	1
O	415	Pearl gray	107	1
✪	902	Garnet−very dark	421	1
V	3820	Straw−dark	231	1

TOP TIPS:

🔘 To turn this pattern into a piece of jewelry, you'll want to wash it thoroughly after you've finished stitching to remove as much starch as possible from the fabric. Then let it air-dry completely. Next, follow these steps:

1. Cut a circle from heavy cardstock or a cereal box that's ever-so-slightly smaller than the inner dimension of your bezel necklace setting (just under a millimeter difference should do the trick).

2. Set this cardstock over your linen crest and, using thread or floss, sew a loose running stitch around about ¾ of an inch wider than the circumference of your cardstock. *Note: If you're new to embroidery, a running stitch is probably exactly what you picture for a traditional stitch: It's a line of small, even stitches, going in and out without overlapping.*

3. Gently pull this thread to cinch the linen fabric around the back of the cardstock. Pause and adjust along the way to make sure the front side shows your house crest perfectly centered. Continue pulling and fitting until you've created a circle that fits neatly around your cardstock.

4. Add additional rows of running stitches as needed, until the fabric lies flat against the cardstock and the edges are even. Trim excess fabric from the folded-back edges as needed.

5. Using tacky craft glue, secure your cardstock circle with the embroidered image face up to the inside of your bezel setting. Remove any excess glue from the linen with a toothpick.

6. Protect the embroidery with waxed paper and place a heavy weight, like a gallon water bottle or several books, on top of it until the glue sets.

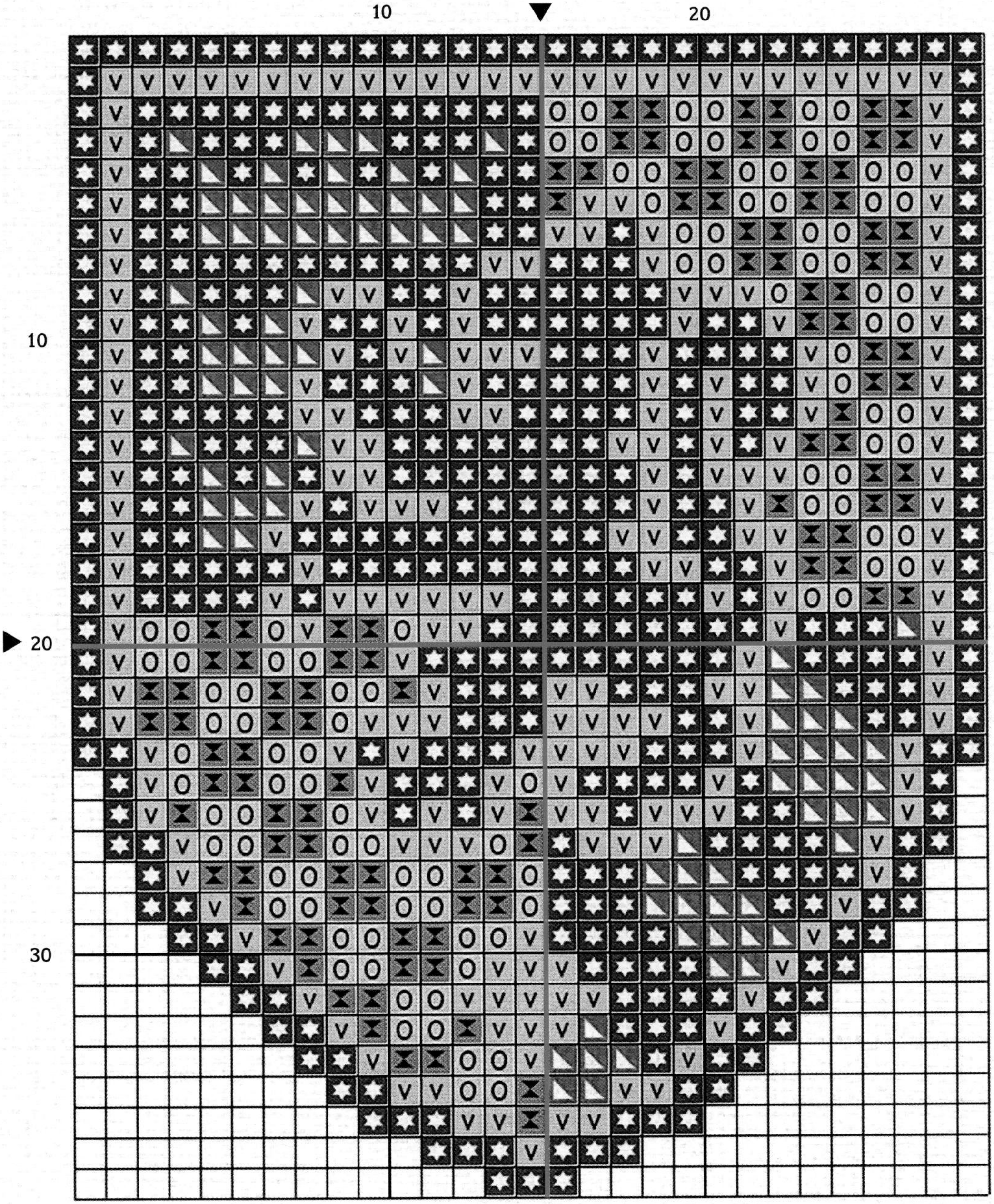
10
20
10
20
30

VIGNETTES

PLATFORM 9¾ AND THE HOGWARTS EXPRESS

PATTERN INFORMATION

- **FABRIC:** 14-count brown Aida, 10 x 8.5 in
- **NEEDLE SIZE:** 24 tapestry needle
- **STITCH COUNT:** 56 x 32
- **FINISHED SIZE:** 4 x 2.3 in
- **MOUNTING:** 4 x 6 in oval hoop, horizontal
- **DIFFICULTY:** Easy

Imagine you've just been given your ticket for the Hogwarts Express, and it says the train departs from Platform 9¾ at King's Cross station. Should be simple to find, right? It's obviously between platforms nine and ten. This challenge is given to Harry Potter in *Harry Potter and the Sorcerer's Stone*, but all he finds between the two platforms is a brick wall! Fortunately, the ginger-haired Weasley family is catching the train at the same time and helps Harry get to the platform, where he sees the Hogwarts Express for the first time.

The Hogwarts Express, which transports new and returning students to the ancient School of Witchcraft and Wizardry every year, is "played" by a locomotive built in 1937 named Olton Hall. It was renamed, with Hogwarts Castle printed on the side and Hogwarts Express on the front. Additionally, the Great Western Railway's standard train color of Brunswick green was changed to maroon. Helicopter shots of the train traveling through Scotland were filmed for exterior views; scenes inside the train were filmed at Leavesden Studios. The cars that carried the students were placed on gimbal rigs that bounced to simulate a train's rocking motion.

Working this pattern is a bit easier than locating a platform for a train that will take you to a school for magic. It combines both the train and the platform number with the excitement of taking your first trip on the Hogwarts Express!

	DMC FLOSS NUMBER	COLOR NAME	NUMBER OF STITICHES IN PATTERN	NUMBER OF STRANDS USED
⊙	4	Tin−dark	45	3
@	152	Shell pink−medium light	20	3
u	168 + White	Pewter−very light + White	83	2 + 1
◻	310	Black	459	3
♠	321	Red	192	3
◩	413	Pewter gray−dark	64	3
▶◀	436	Tan	52	3
◲	646	Beaver gray−dark	228	3
✦	801	Coffee brown−dark	28	3
✳	816	Garnet	144	3
◪	3799	Pewter gray−very dark	78	3
♡	White	White	51	3
—	White	White (backstitching the platform fraction)	1.01	1

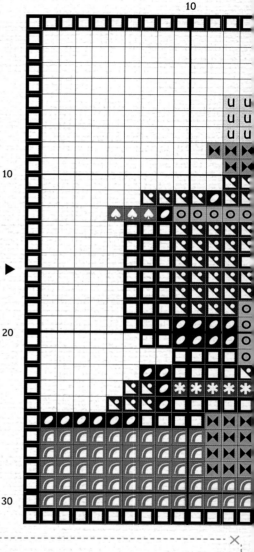

Filming at "Platform 9¾" for *Harry Potter and the Sorcerer's Stone* took place on a Sunday, the least busy day at King's Cross. But when travelers realized the Hogwarts Express was being filmed, a huge crowd gathered. "It was," says director Chris Columbus, "a historic day for Harry Potter fans."

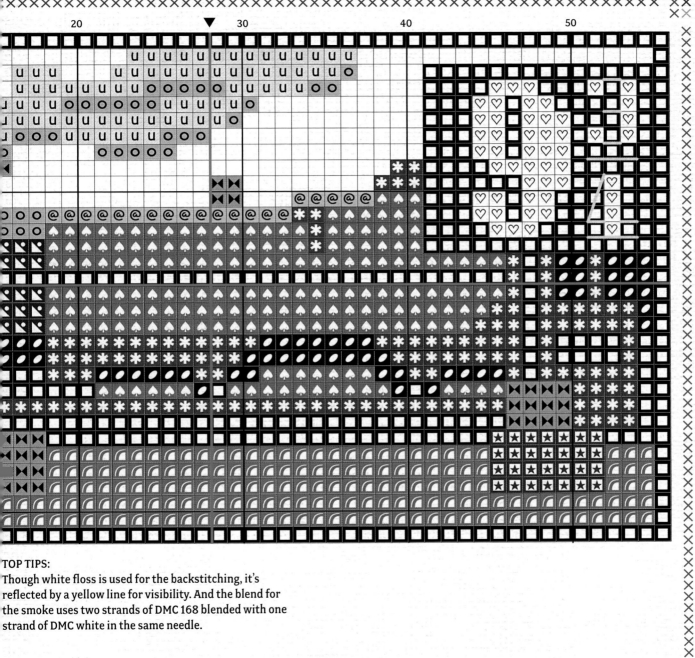

TOP TIPS:
Though white floss is used for the backstitching, it's
reflected by a yellow line for visibility. And the blend for
the smoke uses two strands of DMC 168 blended with one
strand of DMC white in the same needle.

HOGWARTS CASTLE

××

Welcome to Hogwarts! Says production designer Stuart Craig, "An early decision was not to make Hogwarts a fairy-tale castle, but to make it heavy, enduring, and real. The magic, when it did appear, was all the stronger because it was born out of something that was seemingly familiar and real, rather than complete whimsy or complete fantasy." Hogwarts castle was inspired by two of the oldest educational institutions in Britain—Oxford and Cambridge—as well as several of Britain's imposing medieval cathedrals, among them Westminster, Canterbury, and Salisbury. The final result seen in the Harry Potter films was an architectural style based on Medieval Gothic, featuring soaring columns; elaborate carvings; high, pointed arches; and myriad windows.

The iconic and beloved castle itself is lovingly reproduced here in tapestry-style cross-stitch. The sky is formed by the fabric itself, reducing the stitch count to make the project a bit easier. Stitchers can choose any color of blue Aida cloth to suit their personal tastes, from ice blue to navy, or choose a starry sky–print fabric to add extra magic to this project.

PATTERN INFORMATION

- **FABRIC:** 14-count Aida (your choice of celestial print or pale blue), 12 x 10.5 in
- **NEEDLE SIZE:** 24 tapestry needle
- **STITCH COUNT:** 81 x 60
- **FINISHED SIZE:** 5.75 x 4.25 in
- **MOUNTING:** 7 x 5 in oval hoop, horizontal
- **DIFFICULTY:** Easy-Intermediate

Hogwarts castle's profile grew and changed throughout the eight films, but production designer Stuart Craig says nobody seemed to mind: "They seemed to accept that it was part of a magical world."

	DMC FLOSS NUMBER	COLOR NAME	NUMBER OF STITICHES IN PATTERN	NUMBER OF STRANDS USED
□	310	Black	223	3
✖	317	Pewter gray	63	3
▲	318	Steel gray—light	27	3
◣	413	Pewter gray—dark	125	3
◪	648	Beaver gray—light	34	3
♣	801	Coffee brown—dark	10	3
⊖	823	Navy blue—dark	300	3
✱	930	Antique blue—dark	110	3
◥	931	Antique blue—medium	123	3
◪	939	Navy blue—very dark	467	3
8	3041	Antique violet—medium	26	3
⬆	3750	Antique blue—very dark	195	3
◉	3799	Pewter gray—very dark	146	3
◆	3821	Straw	40	3
◧	3838	Lavender blue—dark	36	3
〜	3839	Lavender blue—medium	90	3
5	3840	Lavender blue—light	42	3
●	3841	Pale baby blue	32	3
W	3842	Wedgewood—very dark	71	3
Z	3852	Straw—very dark	46	3
♥	3862	Mocha beige—dark	42	3

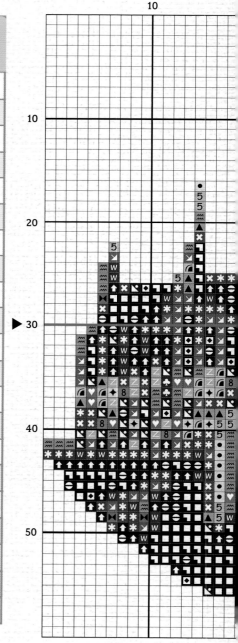

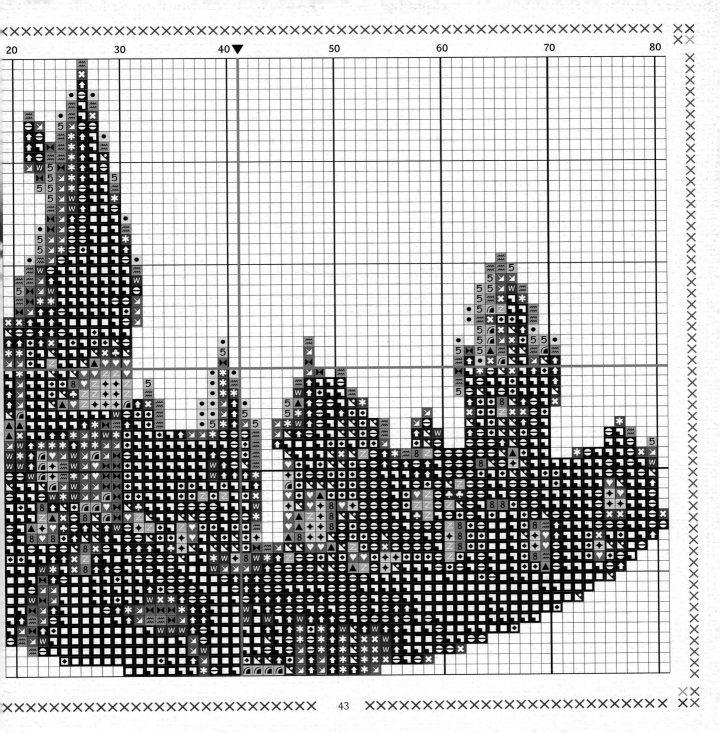

HAGRID'S HUT NIGHT SCENE

✕✕✕✕✕✕✕✕✕✕✕✕✕✕✕✕✕✕✕✕✕✕✕✕✕✕✕✕

Rubeus Hagrid, the Keeper of Keys and Grounds at Hogwarts, lives in a rustic one-room home beside the Forbidden Forest. Hagrid's hut became a place of friendship and safety for Harry Potter and his friends Ron and Hermione. In *Harry Potter and the Prisoner of Azkaban*, Hagrid was named the new Care of Magical Creatures professor, and his hut acquired a second room, which the production designer attributed to his promotion. "We needed a bedroom," says Stuart Craig, "for a story-driven need. So we added a second octagon melded to the first."

The interior of Hagrid's hut was not shot on one set but two! The first set was a huge version of the hut with giant-sized chairs and tables where the young actors were filmed. Then the entire scene was reshot in a smaller version of the hut where everything inside appears in a size proportional to Hagrid's gigantic dimensions.

This piece portrays a peaceful moonlit evening at the cozy home of everyone's favorite half-giant, showing the pumpkin patch that is favored by his Hippogriff, Buckbeak. Some backstitching forms the highlights, which can be worked in silver metallic threads.

PATTERN INFORMATION

- **FABRIC:** 14-count black Aida, 11 x 9 in
- **NEEDLE SIZE:** 24 tapestry needle
- **STITCH COUNT:** 70 x 43
- **FINISHED SIZE:** 5 x 3 in
- **MOUNTING:** 6 x 4 in oval hoop, horizontal
- **DIFFICULTY:** Easy-Intermediate

Everything inside Hagrid's hut, from furniture to mugs to rugs, had to be duplicated in two sizes. First, the set decorators would buy what was needed, then prop makers would create an enlarged version of each item. A London umbrella maker was even commissioned to make Hagrid's pink umbrella wand in two sizes.

	DMC FLOSS NUMBER	COLOR NAME	NUMBER OF STITICHES IN PATTERN	NUMBER OF STRANDS USED
≈	3 + 5200	Tin—medium + Snow white	109	2 + 1
⊠	300	Mahogany—very dark	71	3
✖	317	Pewter gray	125	3
●	318	Steel gray—light	28	3
✳	645	Beaver gray—very dark	42	3
◣	647	Beaver gray—medium	117	3
Ω	648	Beaver gray—light	55	3
○	728	Golden yellow	32	3
⊠	732	Olive green	96	3
◱	838	Beige brown—very dark	73	3
♣	839	Beige brown—dark	100	3
⬆	840	Beige brown—medium	108	3
◪	841	Beige brown—light	86	3
◺	919	Red copper	78	3
⊖	3362	Pine green—dark	133	3
◙	3853	Autumn gold—dark	133	3
♡	5200	Snow white	37	3
—	5283	Silver metallic pearl (backstitching hut and landscape silhouette)	16.21	1

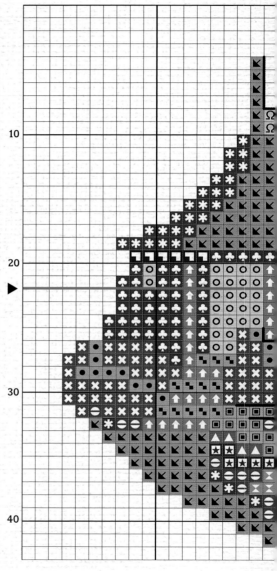

TOP TIP:
The blend for the chimney smoke uses two strands of DMC 3 and one strand of DMC 5200 in the same needle.

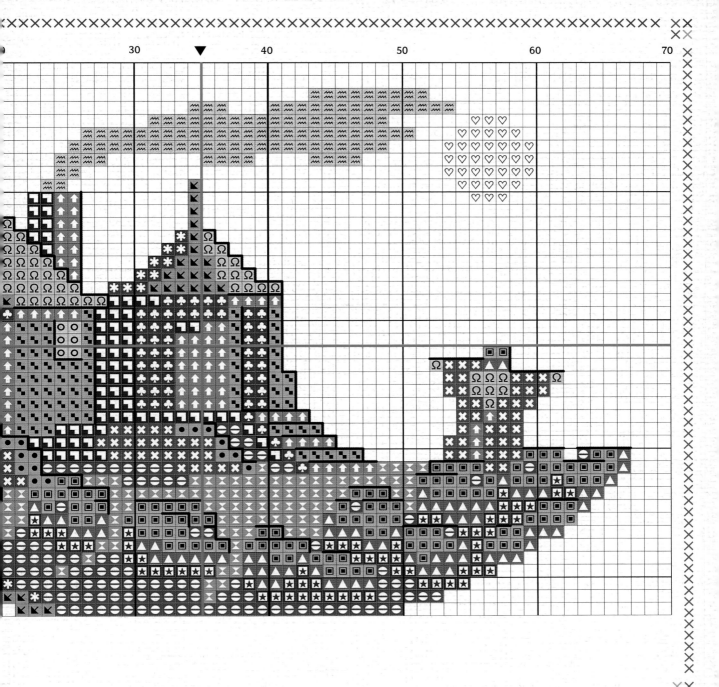

CHAMBER OF SECRETS SNAKE DOOR

XXXXXXXXXXXXXXXXXXXXXXXXXX

The Chamber of Secrets houses a deadly beast—the Basilisk—which is released in Harry's second year to slither through the walls of Hogwarts, Petrifying students and others who view the creature through reflective surfaces in *Harry Potter and the Chamber of Secrets*. The entrance to the Chamber of Secrets is hidden within a sink and sealed off by a locked door featuring eight snakes. Once the password is uttered in Parseltongue, the language of snakes, the door will open.

Visually stunning, the door to the Chamber of Secrets is a real, working mechanical prop designed by special effects supervisor John Richardson and built by special effects supervising engineer Mark Bullimore, who also constructed the doors to the vaults at Gringotts Wizarding Bank. As it opens, seven snakes pull back one by one, wrapping their tails around the door's practical hinge. At the same time, an eighth snake emerges from the bottom and circles around the frame in serpentine waves as the door unlocks.

This pattern's straightforward design is instantly recognizable, even if you're not a Slytherin. With only seven snakes showing, you can rest easy knowing the door remains closed.

PATTERN INFORMATION

- **FABRIC:** 14-count tan Aida, 8 x 9 in
- **NEEDLE SIZE:** 24 tapestry needle
- **STITCH COUNT:** 55 x 54
- **FINISHED SIZE:** 4 x 4 in
- **MOUNTING:** 4 or 5 in round hoop
- **DIFFICULTY:** Easy

	DMC FLOSS NUMBER	COLOR NAME	NUMBER OF STITCHES IN PATTERN	NUMBER OF STRANDS USED
✖	7	Driftwood	389	3
✖	8	Driftwood−dark	318	3
◐	676	Old gold−light	165	3
✕	729	Old gold−medium	212	3
☐	3371	Black brown	185	3
▯	3829	Old gold−very dark	216	3
▣	3863	Mocha beige−medium	821	3

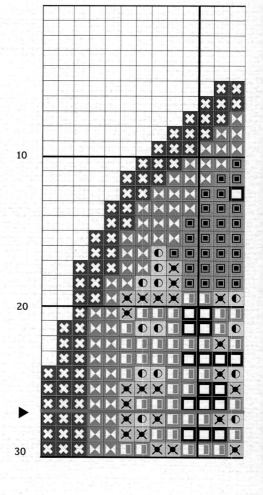

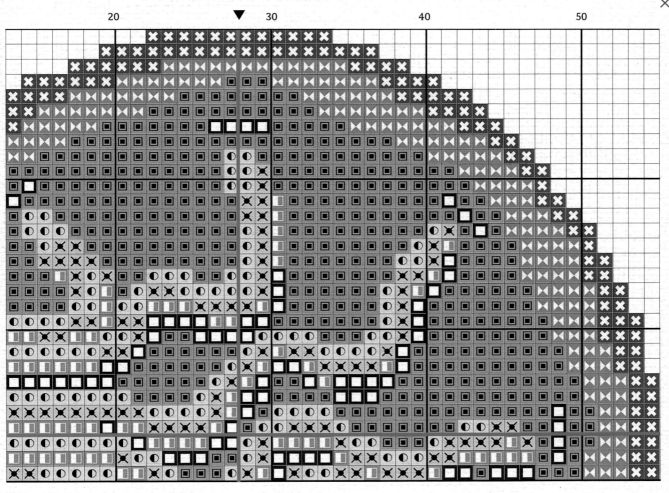

continued on page 52

continued from page 51

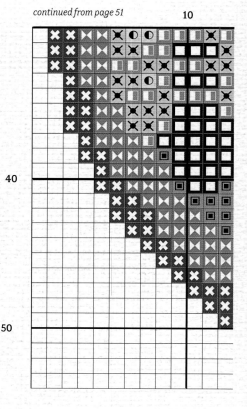

In order to open the door to the Chamber of Secrets, Harry must speak Parseltongue. "It was hard to get a hold on the language at first," says Daniel Radcliffe (Harry), "but I got used to it by the end."

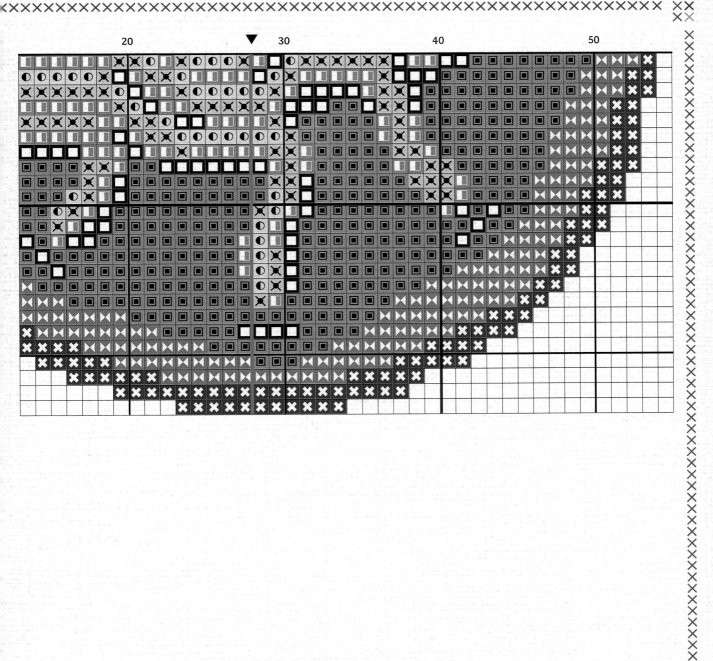

DOLORES UMBRIDGE'S KITTEN PLATE

✕✕✕✕✕✕✕✕✕✕✕✕✕✕✕✕✕✕✕✕✕✕✕✕✕✕

PATTERN INFORMATION

- **FABRIC:** 14-count pink Aida, 12 x 12 in
- **NEEDLE SIZE:** 24 tapestry needle
- **STITCH COUNT:** 85 x 84
- **FINISHED SIZE:** 6 x 6 in
- **MOUNTING:** 6 or 7 in round hoop
- **DIFFICULTY:** Easy-Intermediate

As seen in *Harry Potter and the Order of the Phoenix*, the Defense Against the Dark Arts professor for Harry Potter's fifth year, Dolores Umbridge, is a study in contrasts: her hard-edged, intolerant personality is covered up by a soft, fuzzy, pink wardrobe. She pointedly admits she does not care for children, but shows a great affection for feline friends, evident in the collection of plates featuring cats and kittens that adorn the pink walls in her Hogwarts office.

To create this adorable set decor, forty kittens were filmed playing with a wide selection of kitten-sized props. Crystal balls, a goldfish bowl (with the goldfish mysteriously not there), and a mini motorcycle and sidecar were used for some scenes. There was a beach tableau with sandcastles and seashells, and a field of daisies that held a kitten in a wheelbarrow. And, of course, there were cats wearing witches' hats and sitting in empty cauldrons.

This pattern is a chance to hang your very own kitten plate on the wall, without having to go through Umbridge first. There are a few bits of backstitching for the kitten's features, as well as within the rose petals, bumping this project into a slightly more advanced category.

Dolores Umbridge's Patronus is—no surprise here—a cat. The digital animators gave her Patronus a twitching tail, a pulsating radiance, and even had the cat hiss its displeasure as it prowled around her podium.

	DMC FLOSS NUMBER	COLOR NAME	NUMBER OF STITICHES IN PATTERN	NUMBER OF STRANDS USED
●	162	Blue—ultra very light	4	3
◣	221	Shell pink—very dark	94	3
▢	334	Baby blue—medium	65	3
⌘	500	Blue green—very dark	423	3
◀	502	Blue green	327	3
▯ ◉	502 + 221 + 647	Blue green + Shell pink—very dark + Beaver gray—medium	353	1 + 1 + 1
✳	645	Beaver gray—very dark	99	3
❖	647	Beaver gray—medium	325	3
N	3072	Beaver gray—very light	478	3
⊠	3685	Mauve—dark	67	3
◖	3687	Mauve	444	3
⊃	3688	Mauve—medium	686	3
∞	3865	Winter white	140	3
♡	5200	Snow white	492	3
★	5282	Gold metallic pearl	236	2
—	310	Black (backstitching kitten's eyes and snout)	1.69	1
—	3685	Mauve—dark (backstitching rose petals)	12.5	1

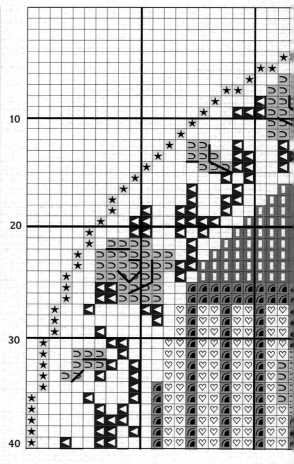

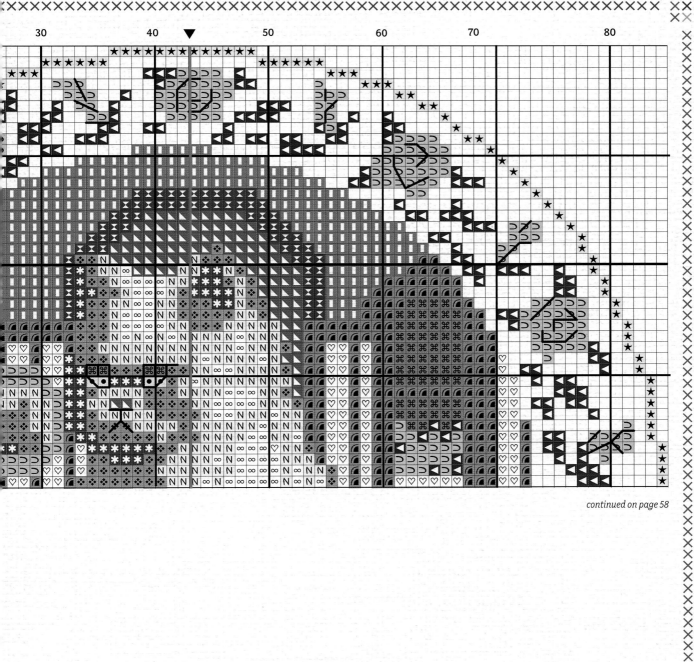

continued on page 58

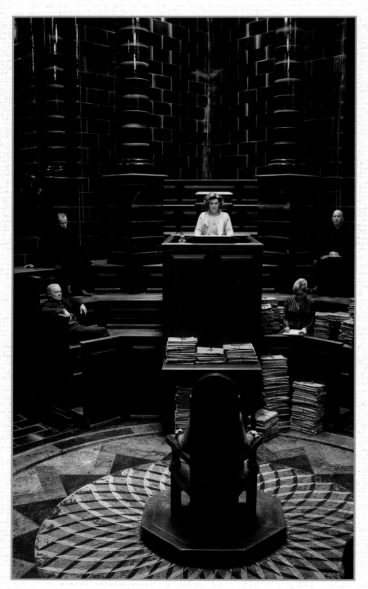

continued from page 57

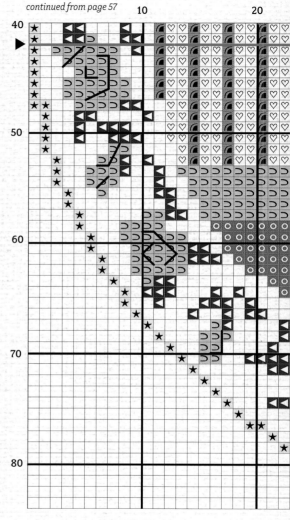

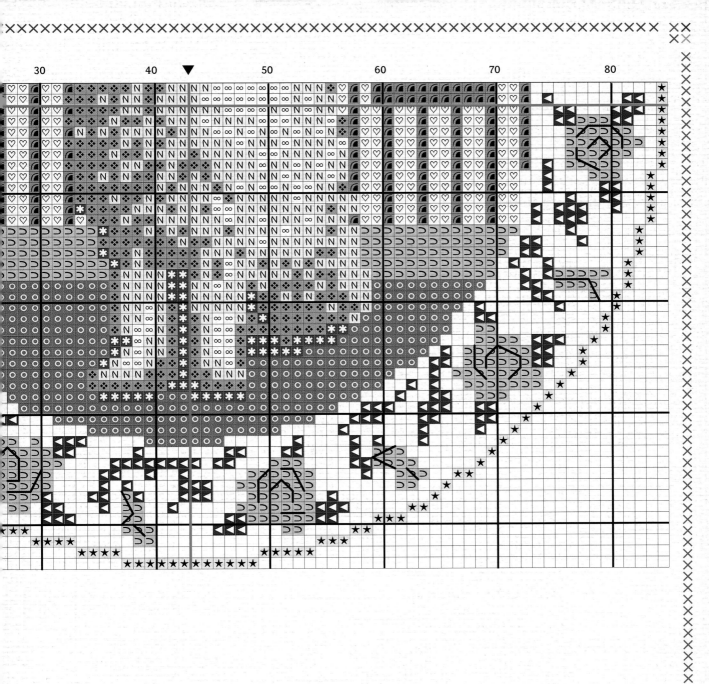

HERMIONE'S TIME-TURNER

×××××××××××××××××××××××××

How many classes is Hermione Granger taking in her third year at Hogwarts? She may say "a fair few," but the truth is it's more than a normal day's schedule would allow, courtesy of a Time-Turner provided to her by Professor Minerva McGonagall in *Harry Potter and the Prisoner of Azkaban.*

Graphic designer Miraphora Mina designed the Time-Turner, wanting to combine the beauty of jewelry with the functionality of a scientific instrument. "I came up with a shape that is a ring within a ring that could lie flat. But I definitely wanted some moving element to be a part of it," says Mina, "so it's really a ring within a ring that opens up and spins."

This piece is as straightforward as they come, giving new stitchers a chance to perfect their technique. And an opportunity to build up skills can be well worth the time; Hermione would probably agree.

PATTERN INFORMATION

- **FABRIC:** 14-count white Aida, 11 x 10 in
- **NEEDLE SIZE:** 24 tapestry needle
- **STITCH COUNT:** 68 x 54
- **FINISHED SIZE:** 5 x 4 in
- **MOUNTING:** 5 in hoop
- **DIFFICULTY:** Easy

	DMC FLOSS NUMBER	COLOR NAME	NUMBER OF STITCHES IN PATTERN	NUMBER OF STRANDS USED
O	168	Pewter—very light	86	3
✖	169	Pewter—light	119	3
V	725	Topaz	895	3
◇	783	Topaz—medium	404	3
●	White	White	32	3
—	801	Coffee brown—dark (backstitching around the golden mechanisms)	81.36	1
—	3799	Pewter gray—very dark (backstitching around the hourglass)	22.5	1

The hourglass inside the Time-Turner is filled with real sand.

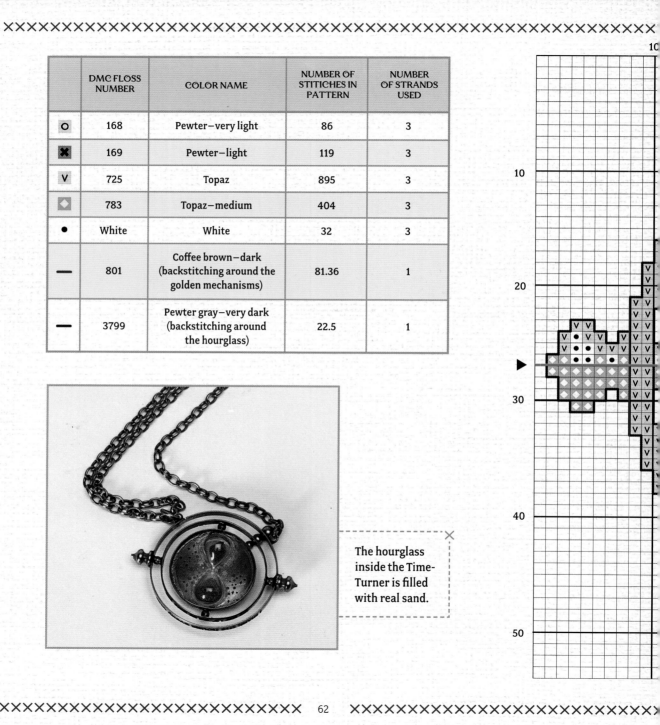

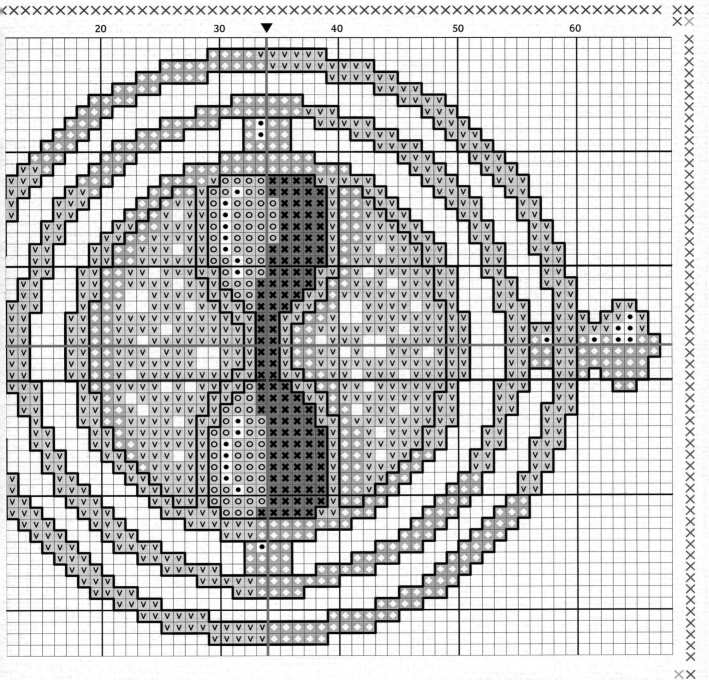

CHARACTERS & CREATURES

HEDWIG

×××××××××××××××

To celebrate Harry's eleventh birthday in *Harry Potter and the Sorcerer's Stone*, Rubeus Hagrid purchases a beautiful snowy owl for him, which Harry names Hedwig. Hedwig is a fiercely loyal friend that provides comfort to the young wizard.

A dozen owls were used throughout the eight Harry Potter films to portray Hedwig, with several trained for specific actions. Elmo, who loved being around people, could sit quietly in a cage or stay on a mark atop a piece of furniture. Wton (which stands for "White Terror of the North") was used mostly for long flying shots. The owl most frequently seen on-screen is Gizmo, who was trained to pick up letters and carry a broomstick in his beak.

Harry's beloved owl Hedwig is depicted on top of one of her favorite perches, Harry's stack of schoolbooks. Stitchers may work this design on a wide variety of color choices, including black, brown, blue, green, oatmeal, ivory, or even a starry sky, and can choose to stitch over two threads on linen if they prefer.

PATTERN INFORMATION

- **FABRIC:** 14-count celestial print or stitcher's choice of color Aida, 10 x 12 in
- **NEEDLE SIZE:** 24 tapestry needle
- **STITCH COUNT:** 59 x 86
- **FINISHED SIZE:** 4.25 x 6.25 in
- **MOUNTING:** 5 x 7 in oval hoop, vertical
- **DIFFICULTY:** Easy-Intermediate

For protection against sharp owl claws, Daniel Radcliffe wore a thick leather guard under his robe when carrying Hedwig.

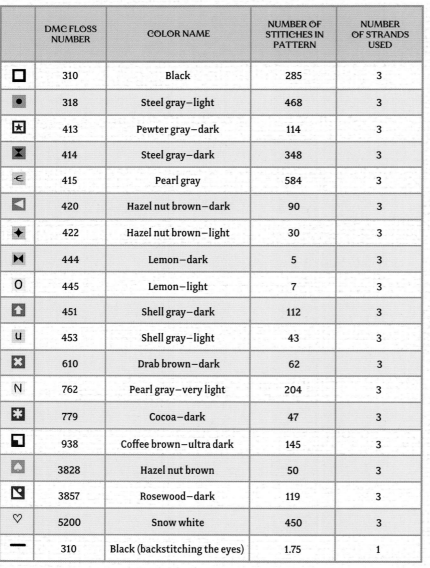

	DMC FLOSS NUMBER	COLOR NAME	NUMBER OF STITCHES IN PATTERN	NUMBER OF STRANDS USED
□	310	Black	285	3
●	318	Steel gray—light	468	3
★	413	Pewter gray—dark	114	3
⬥	414	Steel gray—dark	348	3
∈	415	Pearl gray	584	3
◀	420	Hazel nut brown—dark	90	3
✦	422	Hazel nut brown—light	30	3
⋈	444	Lemon—dark	5	3
O	445	Lemon—light	7	3
⬆	451	Shell gray—dark	112	3
u	453	Shell gray—light	43	3
✖	610	Drab brown—dark	62	3
N	762	Pearl gray—very light	204	3
✳	779	Cocoa—dark	47	3
◗	938	Coffee brown—ultra dark	145	3
⬟	3828	Hazel nut brown	50	3
◥	3857	Rosewood—dark	119	3
♡	5200	Snow white	450	3
—	310	Black (backstitching the eyes)	1.75	1

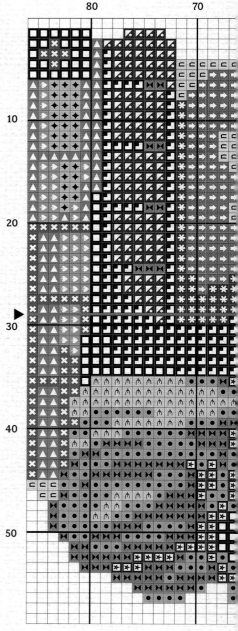

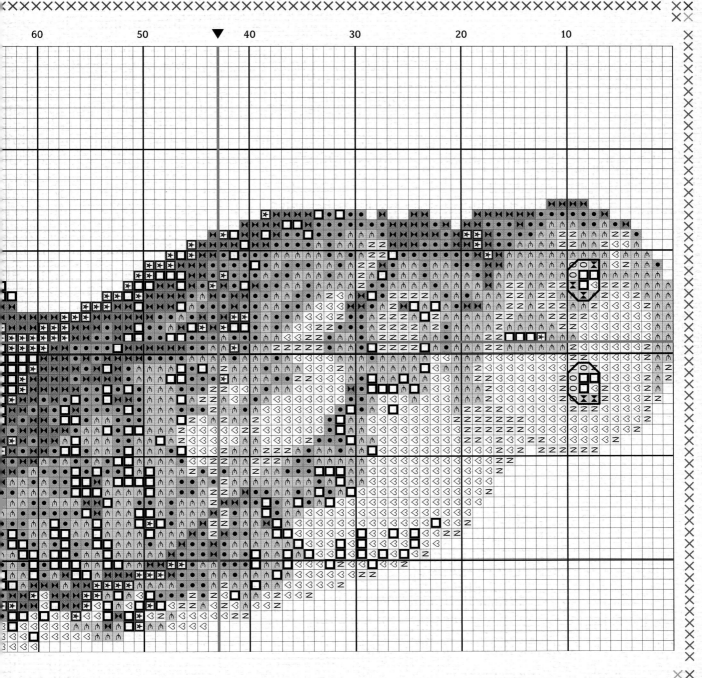

"WHY IS IT ALWAYS YOU THREE" PORTRAIT

×××

PATTERN INFORMATION

- **FABRIC:** 14-count brown Aida, 11.5 x 9.5 in
- **NEEDLE SIZE:** 24 tapestry needle & size 12 sharp sewing needle
- **STITCH COUNT:** 78 x 49
- **FINISHED SIZE:** 5.6 x 3.5 in
- **MOUNTING:** 6 x 4 in oval hoop, horizontal
- **DIFFICULTY:** Intermediate

The name of this piece is a fair observation made by head of Gryffindor house Minerva McGonagall in *Harry Potter and the Half-Blood Prince*. She utters the famous line when Harry, Ron, and Hermione are brought in for questioning after they see fellow Gryffindor Katie Bell cursed by an opal necklace while in Hogsmeade. It's a moment that speaks volumes as McGonagall despairs that once again the trio has been involved in mysterious events.

"Professor McGonagall is very stern," says Dame Maggie Smith, "but I think she needs to be because it's a dangerous game what she's seen, so she keeps a strict eye on [her students], but she's really a softie within the middle."

This tapestry-style portrait shows the trio early and reflects how far they've come together. It includes backstitching to capture details, such as Harry's glasses, and to give their faces more expression than just cross-stitches alone. Note that not all of the background is charted: the brown Aida cloth takes the place of the curtain backdrop of the original scene, which lowers the number of stitches required.

	DMC FLOSS NUMBER	COLOR NAME	NUMBER OF STITICHES IN PATTERN	NUMBER OF STRANDS USED
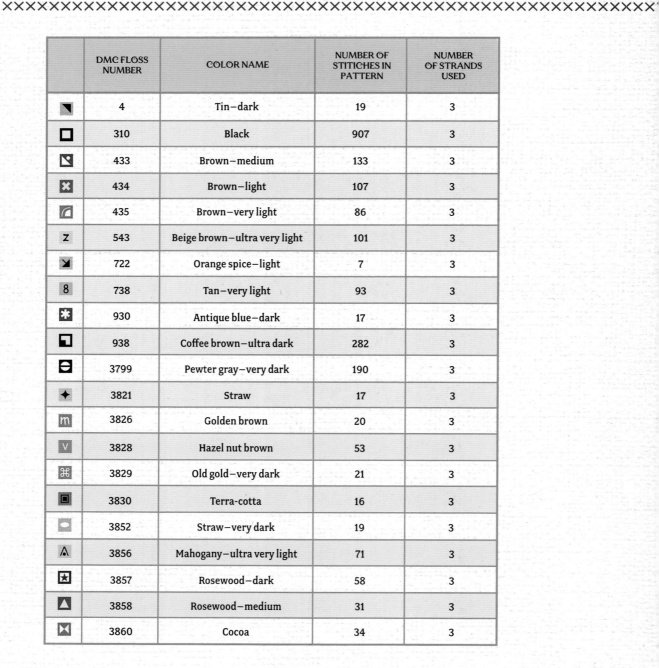	4	Tin—dark	19	3
	310	Black	907	3
	433	Brown—medium	133	3
	434	Brown—light	107	3
	435	Brown—very light	86	3
z	543	Beige brown—ultra very light	101	3
	722	Orange spice—light	7	3
8	738	Tan—very light	93	3
	930	Antique blue—dark	17	3
	938	Coffee brown—ultra dark	282	3
	3799	Pewter gray—very dark	190	3
	3821	Straw	17	3
m	3826	Golden brown	20	3
v	3828	Hazel nut brown	53	3
	3829	Old gold—very dark	21	3
	3830	Terra-cotta	16	3
	3852	Straw—very dark	19	3
A	3856	Mahogany—ultra very light	71	3
	3857	Rosewood—dark	58	3
	3858	Rosewood—medium	31	3
	3860	Cocoa	34	3

	DMC FLOSS NUMBER	COLOR NAME	NUMBER OF STITICHES IN PATTERN	NUMBER OF STRANDS USED
♣	3861	Cocoa—light	23	3
✿	3862	Mocha beige—dark	26	3
≈	3863	Mocha beige—medium	35	3
Ω	3864	Mocha beige—light	42	3
◎	Ecru	Ecru	63	3
—	310	Black (backstitching)	1.13	1
—	433	Brown—medium (backstitching)	0.72	1
—	938	Coffee brown—ultra dark (backstitching)	3.05	1
—	3857	Rosewood—dark (backstitching)	1.31	1

The cursed opal necklace can be seen earlier in a display case at Borgin and Burkes's shop in Knockturn Alley in *Harry Potter and the Chamber of Secrets* with a sign warning not to touch it!

TOP TIPS:
Consider using your traditional size 24 tapestry needle for the majority of the pattern and switching to a small, sharp sewing needle for the delicate backstitching on this one. It'll help you penetrate the fabric and previous stitching.

For backstitching, you could use DMC 310, black floss, throughout. If you prefer a subtle shading effect, we recommend:

- **DMC 310, BLACK:** Harry's eyebrows, Harry's left eye and left side of his glasses, Hermione's left eyebrow and left side of her left eye

- **DMC 433, BROWN MEDIUM:** Ron's eyebrows and eyes

- **DMC 938, COFFEE BROWN ULTRA DARK:** the remainder of Harry's glasses, Hermione's right eyebrow and remainder of her eyes

- **DMC 3857, ROSEWOOD DARK:** Ron's and Harry's noses, lips for all three

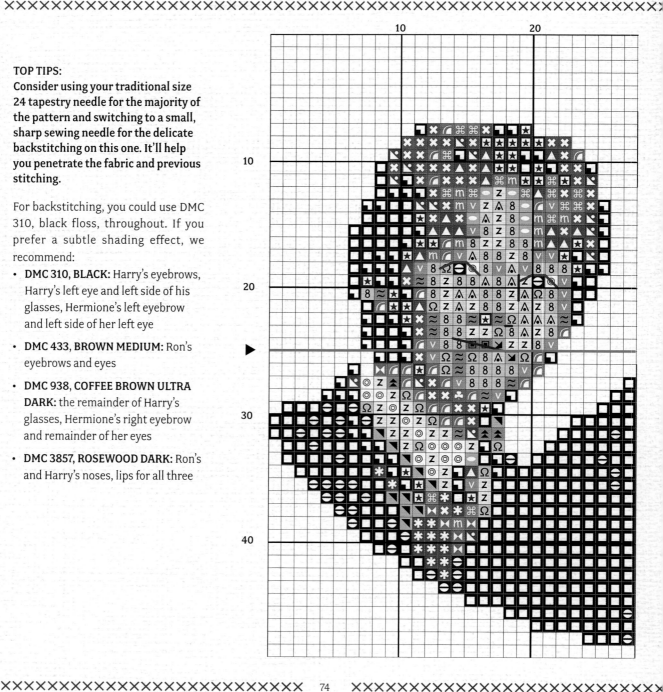

SIRIUS BLACK WANTED POSTER

XXXXXXXXXXXXXXXXXXXXXXXXXXXXXXX

Sirius Black's escape from Azkaban prison sends waves through the wizarding world during Harry Potter's third year at Hogwarts. Framed for murder by his friend Peter Pettigrew, Sirius has waited a long time to break free. Now rumors are that he's coming for Harry, who is also the son of his closest school friend, James.

The wanted poster for Sirius Black, seen in *Harry Potter and the Prisoner of Azkaban*, was created by the graphics department, who decided that the image of Sirius should take up most of the poster. Wanted posters of nineteenth- and twentieth-century outlaws such as Billy the Kid and Bonnie and Clyde were referenced for its style. Then footage of Gary Oldman as a screaming, laughing Sirius was filmed and composited with the static poster. Blue-screen material replaced Sirius's image for live-action filming.

This mug shot of the infamous Azkaban prisoner Sirius Black is rendered entirely in shades of gray. Even though there are no fancy stitches or unusual finishing techniques, tapestry-style patterns can be a bit tricky to count and keep track of, which makes this project more intermediate than easy.

PATTERN INFORMATION

- **FABRIC:** 14-count white Aida, 11 x 12 in
- **NEEDLE SIZE:** 24 tapestry needle
- **STITCH COUNT:** 70 x 76
- **FINISHED SIZE:** 5 x 5.5 in
- **MOUNTING:** 6 in round hoop
- **DIFFICULTY:** Easy-Intermediate

	DMC FLOSS NUMBER	COLOR NAME	NUMBER OF STITICHES IN PATTERN	NUMBER OF STRANDS USED
∴	1	White tin	272	3
ໃ	2	Tin	122	3
8	3	Tin–medium	74	3
✕	4	Tin–dark	71	3
u	168	Pewter–very light	61	3
◰	310	Black	1039	3
●	318	Steel gray–light	108	3
◪	413	Pewter gray–dark	450	3
✖	414	Steel gray–dark	155	3
O	415	Pearl gray	150	3
❯	647	Beaver gray–medium	77	3
◮	3884	Pewter–medium light	306	3
♡	White	White	116	3

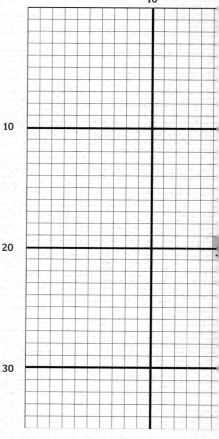

The graphics department added a request on Sirius Black's wanted poster that the Ministry of Magic should be notified by owl with any information that could lead to his arrest.

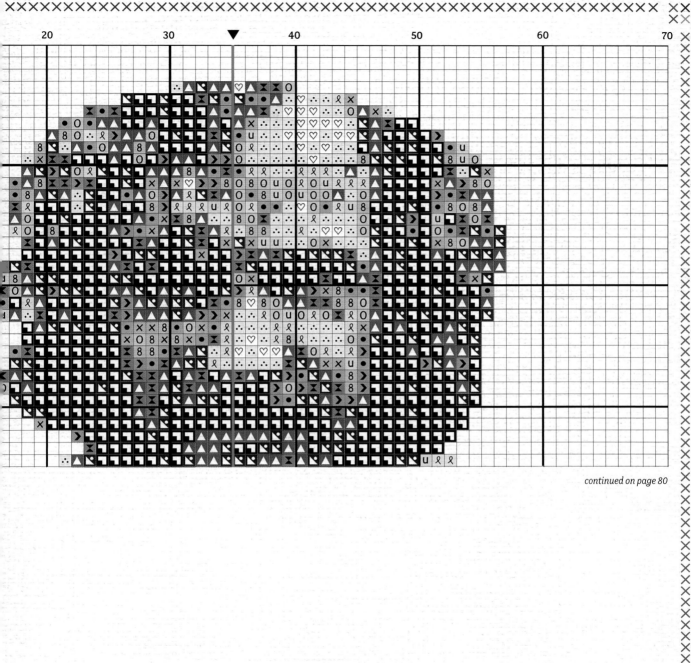

continued on page 80

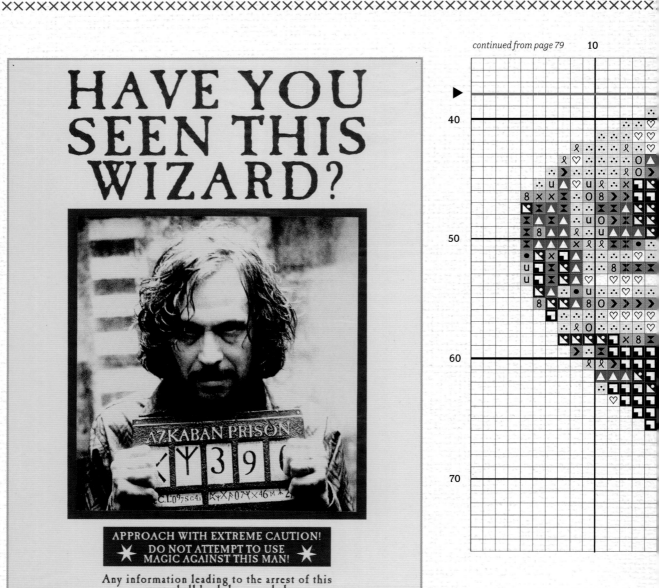

continued from page 79

40

50

60

70

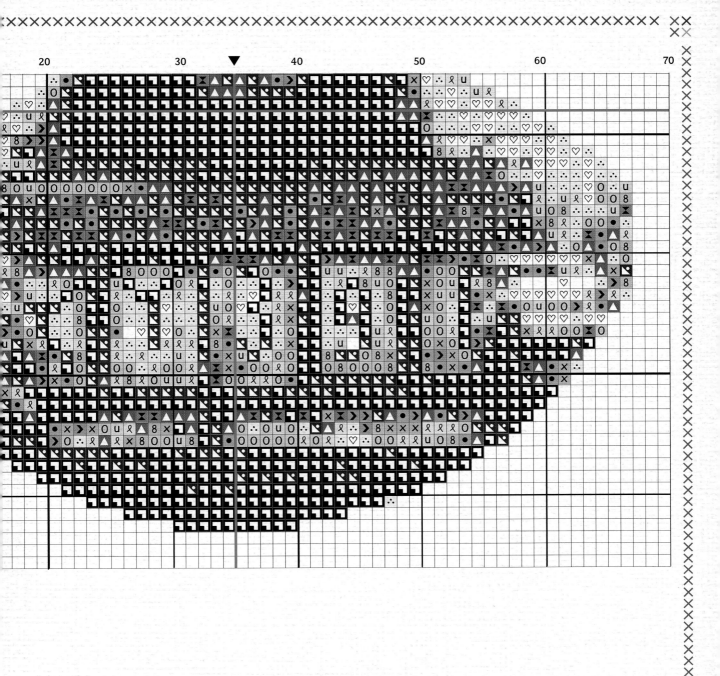

LUNA LOVEGOOD IN SPECTRESPECS

×—×

In *Harry Potter and the Half-Blood Prince*, Harry has a nasty encounter with Draco Malfoy on the Hogwarts Express, leaving Harry stunned by *Petrificus Totalus* and then covered over by his Invisibility Cloak. Fortunately, before the train returns to London, he's discovered by Luna Lovegood. She is wearing a pair of Spectrespecs that help her rescue him, as she can see through the Spectrespecs magical creatures known as Wrackspurts that float around his head. These unique spectacles were available in a special issue of *The Quibbler*, the tabloid-style magazine edited by Luna Lovegood's father.

Typically, *The Quibbler* was printed on thin paper, but this prop's cover was printed on a heavier stock by the graphics department to allow for perforations around the glasses so they could be removed.

Fan-favorite Luna is a real light in the darkness for Harry and his friends. Black Aida is a dramatic contrast to Luna's bright and colorful hues, making her really pop out of the background. Note that black fabric can be more challenging to stitch on than pale colors, so have a good light nearby to help make the holes more visible!

PATTERN INFORMATION

- **FABRIC:** 14-count black Aida, 10 x 12 in
- **NEEDLE SIZE:** 24 tapestry needle
- **STITCH COUNT:** 57 x 70
- **FINISHED SIZE:** 4 x 5 in
- **MOUNTING:** 4 x 6 in oval hoop, vertical
- **DIFFICULTY:** Intermediate

Graphic designer Miraphora Mina was inspired by 1960s pop art for the "eye-catching" Spectrespecs.

	DMC FLOSS NUMBER	COLOR NAME	NUMBER OF STITCHES IN PATTERN	NUMBER OF STRANDS USED
☌	23	Apple blossom	16	3
♥	99	Variegated mauve	369	3
↑	152	Shell pink—medium light	94	3
✕	162	Blue—ultra very light	16	3
◎	223	Shell pink—light	105	3
8	224	Shell pink—very light	107	3
△	225	Shell pink—ultra very light	71	3
⛰	315	Antique mauve—medium dark	147	3
★	550	Violet—very dark	1	3
W	676	Old gold—light	218	3
♠	718	Plum	12	3
⌘	729	Old gold—medium	212	3
⊖	934	Black avocado green	296	3
◪	938	Coffee brown—ultra dark	23	3
✳	995	Electric blue—dark	1	3
❯	996	Electric blue—medium	4	3
♣	3362	Pine green—dark	161	3
Z	3823	Yellow—ultra pale	147	3
✚	3829	Old gold—very dark	175	3
◣	3858	Rosewood—medium	35	3

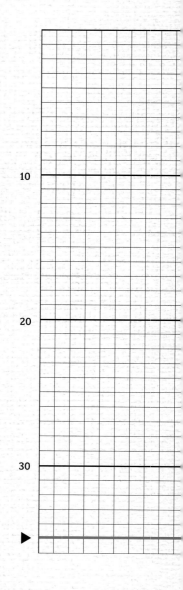

TOP TIP:
For Luna's jacket, try using a "confetti" technique. This means making each stitch of the variegated floss in a random location within the color area until the areas are filled in.

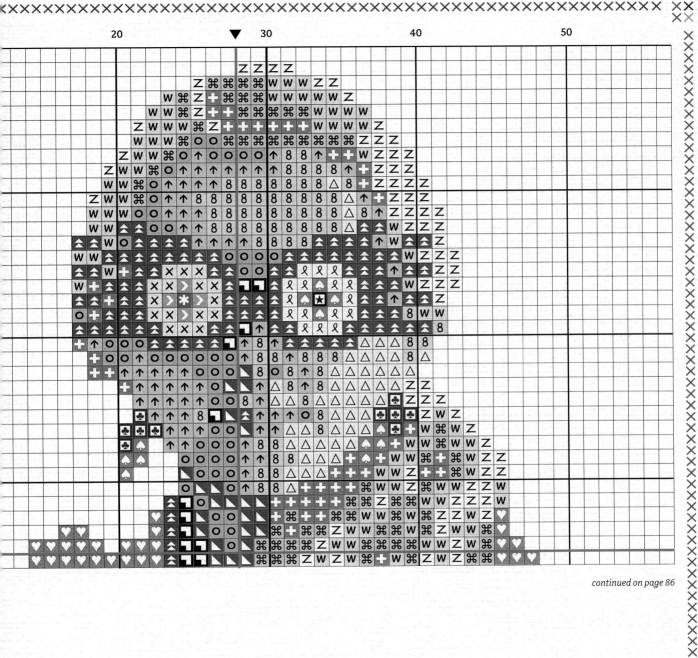

continued on page 86

continued from page 85

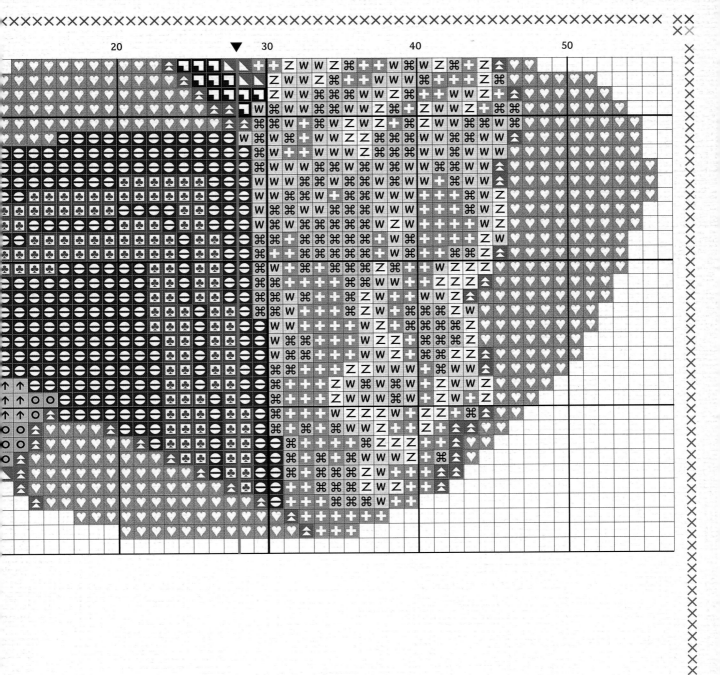

POTTED MANDRAKE ROOT

×××

PATTERN INFORMATION

- **FABRIC:** 28-count khaki linen, 9 x 11 in
- **NEEDLE SIZE:** 24 tapestry needle
- **STITCH COUNT:** 36 x 65
- **FINISHED SIZE:** 2.6 x 4.7 in
- **MOUNTING:** 4 x 6 in oval hoop, vertical
- **DIFFICULTY:** Easy

Harry Potter's second-year Herbology class provided a crucial lesson in repotting Mandrakes—screeching, squirming plants that create the Mandrake Restorative Draught for those who have been Petrified. But first, they have to deal with the wriggling, writhing things in *Harry Potter and the Chamber of Secrets*.

More than fifty completely animatronic Mandrakes were created by the creature shop. Inside their flowerpots was machinery that would cause the top half of their bodies to squirm and wiggle. Controllers who sat under the massive wooden table in the middle of Greenhouse Three could make them go faster or slower. A few Mandrakes could be removed from their flowerpots, move their arms and mouths, and even bite Draco Malfoy's finger!

There are no fancy threads or backstitching on this project, so it's as easy and relaxing as a screaming plant can be. It may be stitched as usual over 14-count fiddler's cloth (which is essentially a rustic-looking Aida) or over two threads on 28-count linen (equivalent to 14-count Aida).

	DMC FLOSS NUMBER	COLOR NAME	NUMBER OF STITICHES IN PATTERN	NUMBER OF STRANDS USED
⌘	356	Terra-cotta—medium	86	3
✖	434	Brown—light	9	3
Ж	642	Beige gray—dark	114	3
O	758	Terra-cotta—very light	201	3
6	772	Yellow green—very light	129	3
◆	895	Hunter green—very dark	100	3
✳	975	Golden brown—dark	12	3
◨	976	Golden brown—medium	5	3
★	3021	Brown gray—very dark	135	3
◑	3346	Hunter green	240	3
5	3782	Mocha brown—light	75	3
◀	3790	Beige gray—ultra dark	118	3
▣	3830	Terra-cotta	109	3

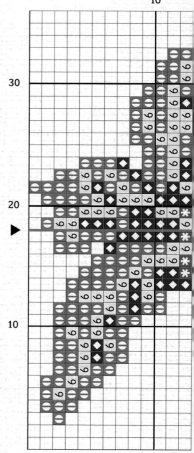

The creature designers didn't want to make the Mandrakes too cute as they knew they would be destroyed to make the Mandrake Restorative Draught.

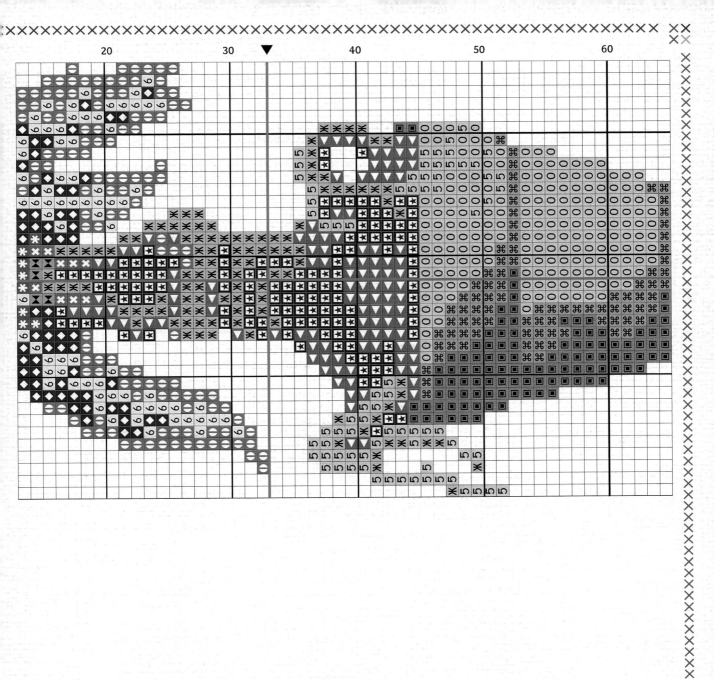

THE MONSTER BOOK OF MONSTERS

When Rubeus Hagrid is named the new Care of Magical Creatures professor in *Harry Potter and the Prisoner of Azkaban*, he assigns *The Monster Book of Monsters* for his class curriculum. The class's first challenge is in opening the book itself (students need to stroke its spine).

Graphic designer Miraphora Mina developed several versions of *The Monster Book of Monsters*. One had clawed feet, and another had a tail. Sometimes the book had two eyes, sometimes four, and they were never in the same place on the cover. Fur, snaggly teeth, and tentacles were added in the final design, with the tome's ribbon bookmark becoming its tongue.

Once finalized, mechanical iterations of the book were created: one to be held in the students' hands with radio-controlled moving tentacles, and another with a snapping mouth that spewed out shredded paper.

Make this stitched version of the strangest textbook ever, then add four tiny toy eyes for the monstrous finishing touch. Stitchers blend two different colors of floss in the same needle to give it a heather look that simulates the fur of the original book.

PATTERN INFORMATION

- **FABRIC:** 14-count ecru or light oatmeal Aida, 10 x 10 in
- **NEEDLE SIZE:** 24 tapestry needle
- **STITCH COUNT:** 56 x 50
- **FINISHED SIZE:** 4 x 3.6 in
- **MOUNTING:** 5 in hoop
- **ADDITIONAL MATERIAL:** doll eyes, yellow or amber glass, two 3mm and two 4mm
- **DIFFICULTY:** Easy

	DMC FLOSS NUMBER	COLOR NAME	NUMBER OF STITCHES IN PATTERN	NUMBER OF STRANDS USED
☐	310	Black	14	3
o	543	Beige brown—ultra very light	39	3
◐	645 + 3021	Beaver gray—very dark + Brown gray	113	1 + 2
⬆	840	Beige brown—medium	58	3
▽	840 + 647	Beige brown—medium + Beaver gray—medium	132	2 + 1
◤	902	Garnet—very dark	16	3
◪	938	Coffee brown—ultra dark	74	3
⋈	3726	Antique mauve—dark	15	3
✳	3802	Antique mauve—very dark	23	3
▣	3863 + 647	Mocha beige—medium + Beaver gray—medium	1138	2 + 1
➕	3863	Mocha beige—medium	14	3
Ω	3864	Mocha beige—light	47	3
⅄	Ecru	Ecru	22	3

TOP TIPS:
Use two 3mm and two 4mm yellow or amber glass doll eyes for *The Monster Book of Monsters*'s eyes. Plunge the slim metal wire through the center of the four dark areas in the middle of the book, then use needle-nose pliers to carefully bend the wire at a 90-degree angle on the back of the embroidery to secure each eye in place.

The Monster Book of Monsters has several pages of text inside it, written by the graphic designer. It's also filled with images of creatures, such as a house-elf and Mandrake, drawn by the concept artists.

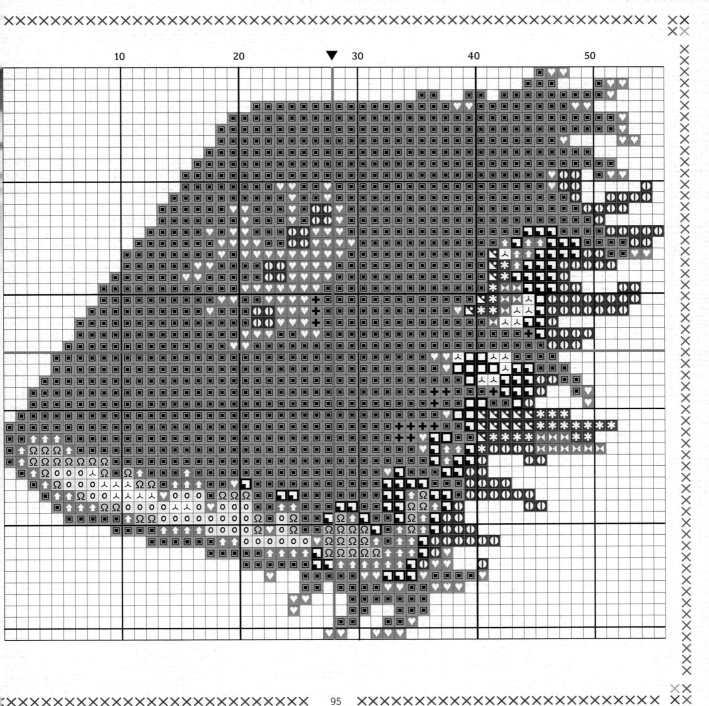

DOBBY IS A FREE ELF

Harry Potter's interactions with Dobby the house-elf in *Harry Potter and the Chamber of Secrets* do not start out positive. First, Dobby drops a cake on the head of Harry's uncle's house guest, then he enchants a Bludger to hit Harry in Quidditch. But Dobby's intentions are honorable: he serves the Malfoy family and knows they intend to harm Harry. As a thank-you for these perhaps misguided but well-meaning attempts to save his life, Harry tricks Lucius Malfoy into giving Dobby a sock. When a master hands their house-elf a piece of clothing, they are set free!

Dobby is the film series' first fully computer-generated major character. The first time Jason Isaacs, who plays Lucius Malfoy, acted in a scene with Dobby, he recalls asking: "Where is Dobby going to be in the room? Where should I look? And I was told, 'Well, wherever you look, that's where we'll put him.'"

Naturally, a sock-shaped silhouette frames Dobby in this tapestry-style portrait. The limited color palette and largely solid background that forms the sock shape make stitching a bit easier for newer crafters. And there's actually a full pair of socks in this project—Dobby's holding the one that granted him freedom.

PATTERN INFORMATION

- **FABRIC:** 14-count white Aida, 9.5 x 12 in
- **NEEDLE SIZE:** 24 tapestry needle
- **STITCH COUNT:** 46 x 85
- **FINISHED SIZE:** 3.3 x 6 in
- **MOUNTING:** 4 x 6 in oval hoop, vertical
- **DIFFICULTY:** Easy

Actor Jason Isaacs (Lucius Malfoy) remembers that when young visitors to the set asked to meet Dobby, he would tell them the house-elf was in his trailer or not on set that day.

	DMC FLOSS NUMBER	COLOR NAME	NUMBER OF STITICHES IN PATTERN	NUMBER OF STRANDS USED
⊃	164	Forest green–light	99	3
☐	310	Black	58	3
◩	355	Terra cotta–dark	76	3
♣	645	Beaver gray–very dark	37	3
◆	646	Beaver gray–dark	140	3
Ω	648	Beaver gray–light	220	3
✳	779	Cocoa–dark	63	3
⋀	950	Desert sand–light	308	3
◥	986	Forest green–very dark	165	3
▥	997	Forest green–dark	413	3
⬆	988	Forest green – medium	252	3
✕	989	Forest green	161	3
r	3072	Beaver gray–very light	122	3
∃	3774	Desert sand–very light	62	3
o	3778	Terra cotta–light	27	3
▲	3861	Cocoa–light	159	3
∞	3865	Winter white	14	3
—	355	Terra cotta – dark (backstitching mouth and eyes)	3.3	1

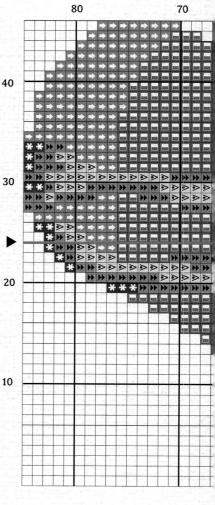

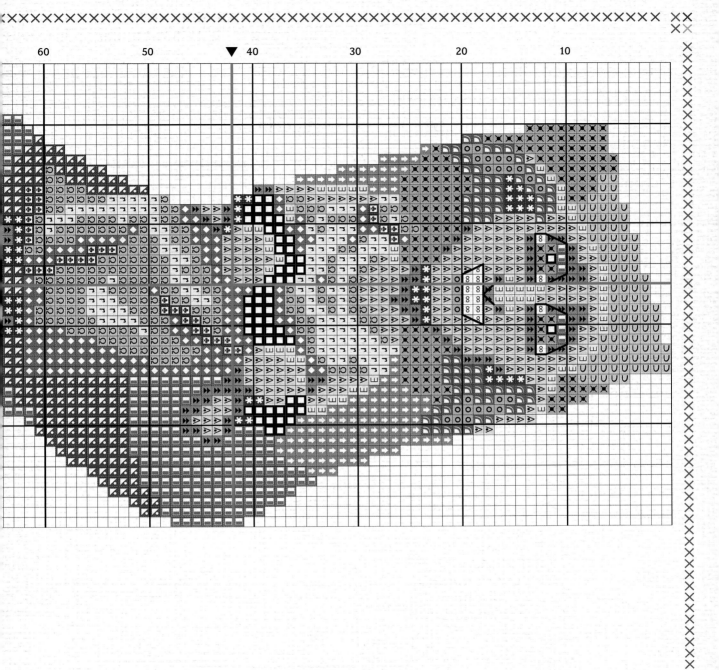

FAWKES THE PHOENIX

××××××××××××××××××××××××××

The trusted companion of Hogwarts Headmaster Albus Dumbledore's is a phoenix named Fawkes. Phoenixes are immortal birds that go through three stages of life—at the end of the last stage, they burst into fire and are then reborn from the ashes. Harry is fortunate to witness this transformation upon his first meeting with Fawkes in Dumbledore's office in *Harry Potter and the Chamber of Secrets*.

When it came to Fawkes's design, the choice of coloring was an easy one: It had to be fiery, with a palette of burnt oranges and dark reds. His underside is rendered in shades of gold, as birds have darker colors on their tops than their bellies. Fawkes's neck and throat are variegated oranges with a gold trim. The older Fawkes, who Harry meets on what is called a Burning Day, was given the coloring of a "burnt-out match," says concept artist Adam Brockbank, "but there are still the last embers of brightness about his eyes." Baby Fawkes's coloring combines the gray of the ashes he emerges from with a washed-out pinkish red.

This fantastic creature, in the height of his life, shimmers in the light of Dumbledore's study, courtesy of DMC gold metallic pearl.

PATTERN INFORMATION

- **FABRIC:** 14-count brown Aida, 10 x 12 in
- **NEEDLE SIZE:** 24 tapestry needle
- **STITCH COUNT:** 57 x 84
- **FINISHED SIZE:** 4 x 6 in
- **MOUNTING:** 5 x 6 in oval hoop, vertical
- **DIFFICULTY:** Intermediate

"One of the most wonderful moments I remember was Richard Harris [Albus Dumbledore] walking up to Fawkes and thinking it was a real bird," says Daniel Radcliffe, who portrays Harry Potter. "Absolutely, 100 percent, believing it."

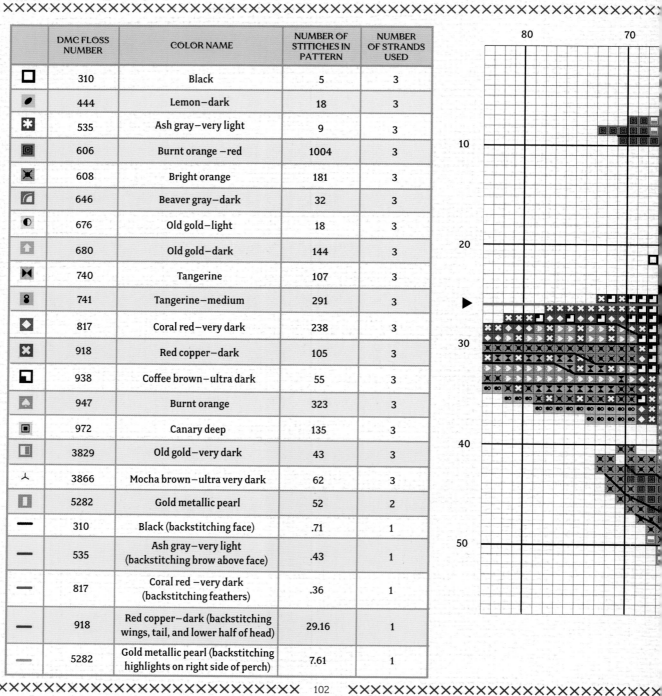

	DMC FLOSS NUMBER	COLOR NAME	NUMBER OF STITCHES IN PATTERN	NUMBER OF STRANDS USED
☐	310	Black	5	3
●	444	Lemon–dark	18	3
✳	535	Ash gray–very light	9	3
◙	606	Burnt orange –red	1004	3
✖	608	Bright orange	181	3
◿	646	Beaver gray–dark	32	3
◐	676	Old gold–light	18	3
⬆	680	Old gold–dark	144	3
▶◀	740	Tangerine	107	3
8	741	Tangerine–medium	291	3
◆	817	Coral red–very dark	238	3
✖	918	Red copper–dark	105	3
◳	938	Coffee brown–ultra dark	55	3
◭	947	Burnt orange	323	3
▣	972	Canary deep	135	3
◨	3829	Old gold–very dark	43	3
人	3866	Mocha brown–ultra very dark	62	3
◧	5282	Gold metallic pearl	52	2
—	310	Black (backstitching face)	.71	1
—	535	Ash gray–very light (backstitching brow above face)	.43	1
—	817	Coral red –very dark (backstitching feathers)	.36	1
—	918	Red copper–dark (backstitching wings, tail, and lower half of head)	29.16	1
—	5282	Gold metallic pearl (backstitching highlights on right side of perch)	7.61	1

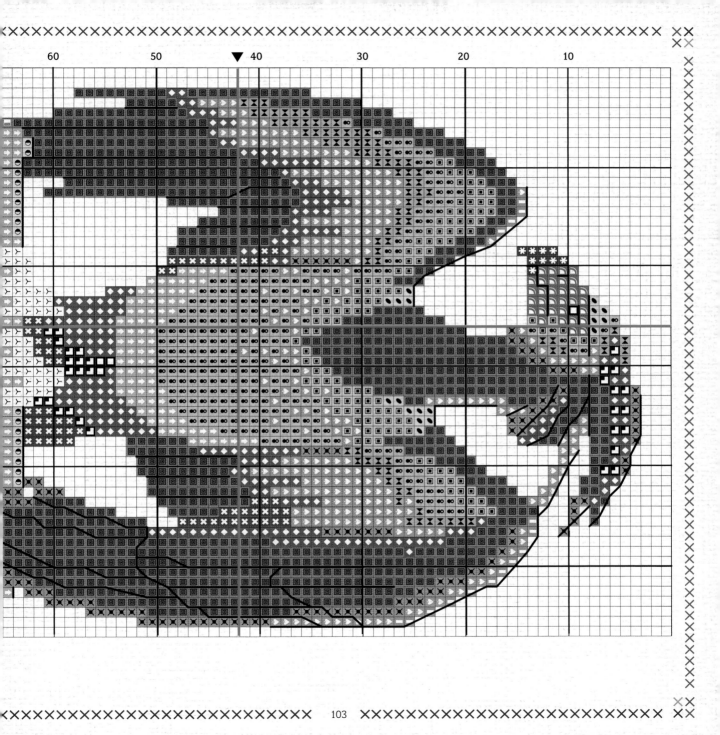

ENCHANTING EPHEMERA

BOOKMARKS

Headmaster Albus Dumbledore, Professor Minerva McGonagall, Professor Rubeus Hagrid, and Professor Severus Snape make up these paper-based bookmarks, perfect to use in any tome you're reading to save your place. Another bookmark is based on the Dueling Club formed by Gilderoy Lockhart in *Harry Potter and the Chamber of Secrets* and rounds out this collection of lovely page savers.

Books abound in the journey of Harry Potter, from the Restricted Section in the Hogwarts library to the many books Hermione brings with her as the trio of friends pursues Horcruxes. For the gravity-defying books in Flourish and Blotts in Diagon Alley, fake books had holes drilled in them so they could be strung on a curved metal bar like beads. Textbooks were created by the graphics department for all the Hogwarts classes, including *A Beginner's Guide to Transfiguration* for Professor McGonagall, *The Monster Books of Monsters* for Hagrid's Care of Magical Creatures, and *Advanced Potion-Making* for the sixth-year Potions professor, Horace Slughorn.

Each of these professorial bookmarks has a stylized design to make stitching a snap. Simply cut out around the finished shape and you're done!

ALBUS DUMBLEDORE BOOKMARK

XXXXXXXXXXXXXXXXXXXXXXXXXXXXXXXXXXXXXXXXX

PATTERN INFORMATION

- **FABRIC:** 14-count white perforated paper, 2 x 6 in
- **NEEDLE SIZE:** 24 tapestry needle
- **STITCH COUNT:** 21 x 70
- **FINISHED SIZE:** 1.5 x 5 in
- **MOUNTING:** N/A
- **DIFFICULTY:** Easy

After the sad passing of Headmaster Albus Dumbledore in *Harry Potter and the Half-Blood Prince, Daily Prophet* reporter Rita Skeeter writes a tell-all biography of him, later read by Hermione for clues to the Deathly Hallows in *Harry Potter and the Deathly Hallows – Part 1*. The book needed to be as frothy and flashy as the reporter. Graphic artists Miraphora Mina and Eduardo Lima were "absolutely stunned," says Mina, "because, in this world, how could we print something so artificial? But we already knew how gaudy and salacious the character was. She's sensational, so with the design of this book we chose to do that by using really artificial colors, techniques, and finishes."

The thinnest paper possible was used in the construction of the book for it to appear cut-rate compared to the beautiful, leatherbound books normally seen in the wizarding world. The front cover's graphic burst and spine border is in an acid-green color that matches the outfit Skeeter is wearing on the back (her first costume in *Harry Potter and the Goblet of Fire*).

This version of Albus Dumbledore is from *Harry Potter and the Prisoner of Azkaban*, where the headmaster tied together his beard with a little chain.

	DMC FLOSS NUMBER	COLOR NAME	NUMBER OF STITCHES IN PATTERN	NUMBER OF STRANDS USED
☐	8	Driftwood—dark	17	3
▲	169	Pewter—light	3	3
✕	543	Beige brown—ultra very light	93	3
♥	3752	Antique blue—very light	1025	3
○	White	White	226	3

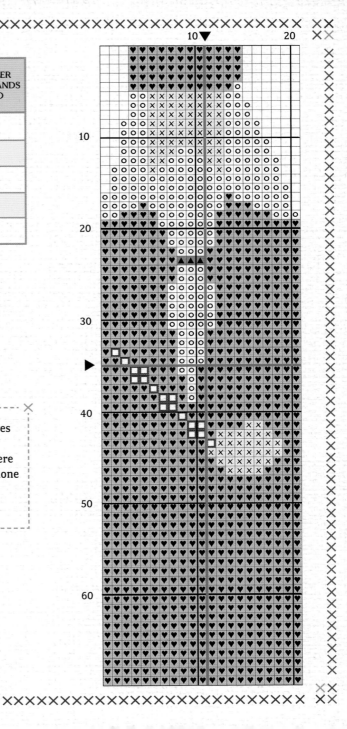

The books on the shelves of Headmaster Albus Dumbledore's office were actually old London phone directories covered in paper and dust.

TOP TIP:
Remember that the back will be visible for this one! To keep it as neat as possible, try running loose threads through previous stitching.

MINERVA MCGONAGALL BOOKMARK

×××××××××××××××××××××××××××

PATTERN INFORMATION

- **FABRIC:** 14-count white perforated paper, 2 x 6 in
- **NEEDLE SIZE:** 24 tapestry needle
- **STITCH COUNT:** 21 x 70
- **FINISHED SIZE:** 1.5 x 5 in
- **MOUNTING:** N/A
- **DIFFICULTY:** Easy

Head of Gryffindor house Minerva McGonagall is the professor for Transfiguration—the ability for one object to be transformed into another. In her class for second years, in *Harry Potter and the Chamber of Secrets*, McGonagall transforms a horn-billed bird into a water goblet with the spell *Vera Verto*. (Ron Weasley does not do so well with his broken wand, transfiguring his rat, Scabbers, into a goblet with both brown fur and a tail.)

The graphic design department handcrafted books for each Harry Potter film, with a minimum of thirty-six copies of each textbook required for each class. An additional five to eight duplicates were needed for any schoolbook used by a main character, in case of damage. Books where pages would be seen on-screen were bound with roughly twenty sheets of text, repeated until the desired thickness was reached. The graphic design department, headed by Miraphora Mina and Eduardo Lima, also provided the written text used for each bound book.

Professor McGonagall is dressed in her greenest green robe in this project—a color actor Dame Maggie Smith insisted for her character's wardrobe, as she told the costume designer that McGonagall's Scottish roots must never be forgotten.

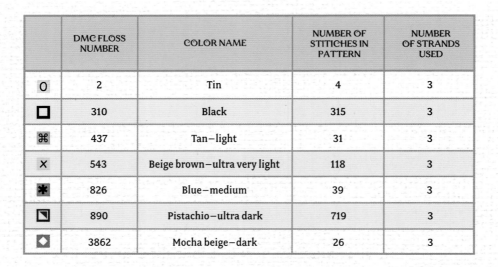

	DMC FLOSS NUMBER	COLOR NAME	NUMBER OF STITICHES IN PATTERN	NUMBER OF STRANDS USED
O	2	Tin	4	3
□	310	Black	315	3
⌘	437	Tan—light	31	3
✕	543	Beige brown—ultra very light	118	3
✳	826	Blue—medium	39	3
◩	890	Pistachio—ultra dark	719	3
◈	3862	Mocha beige—dark	26	3

The author's names for books that weren't already in the original Harry Potter novels came from friends, family, or members of the graphics department. *Olde and Forgotten Bewitchments and Charms* is by E. Limus (Eduardo Lima), *Ancient Runes Made Easy* is by Laurenzoo (Lauren Wakefield), and *New Theory of Numerology* is by Lukos Karzos (Miraphora Mina's son).

TOP TIP:
Remember that the back will be visible for this one! To keep it as neat as possible, try running loose threads through previous stitching.

RUBEUS HAGRID BOOKMARK

×××××××××××××××××××××××××××××××

In addition to the course book *The Monster Book of Monsters*, assigned by Care of Magical Creatures professor Rubeus Hagrid to his students in *Harry Potter and the Prisoner of Azkaban*, there were many other books about creatures great and small in the wizarding world seen throughout the Harry Potter films. In Flourish and Blotts book shop on Diagon Alley, first seen at Gilderoy Lockhart's book signing in *Harry Potter and the Chamber of Secrets*, there are several sections wholly dedicated to creatures, with signage created by the graphics department pointing to Batologies, Owlologies, and Dragons.

Perhaps the most famous book on creatures is Newt Scamander's *Fantastic Beasts and Where to Find Them*. A contemporary version of the book was created for *Harry Potter and the Sorcerer's Stone*, as the book was required for first years at Hogwarts. Graphic designers Miraphora Mina and Eduardo Lima rethought the design of the book for its first publication in the art deco era of the 1920s, when Newt's book was first published.

Even Hagrid's big hands would be adept at stitching this pattern, as there's a lot of beard to handle. The only addition Hagrid would have probably liked for this would be adding an image of a dragon!

PATTERN INFORMATION

- **FABRIC:** 14-count white perforated paper, 2 x 6 in
- **NEEDLE SIZE:** 24 tapestry needle
- **STITCH COUNT:** 21 x 70
- **FINISHED SIZE:** 1.5 x 5 in
- **MOUNTING:** N/A
- **DIFFICULTY:** Easy

	DMC FLOSS NUMBER	COLOR NAME	NUMBER OF STITICHES IN PATTERN	NUMBER OF STRANDS USED
O	2	Tin	13	3
☐	310	Black	123	3
✦	422	Hazel nut brown–light	7	3
♣	433	Brown–medium	179	3
✗	543	Beige brown–ultra very light	78	3
✹	839	Beige brown–dark	23	3
◼	841	Beige brown–light	574	3
★	3781 + 169	Mocha brown–dark + Pewter–light	432	2 + 1

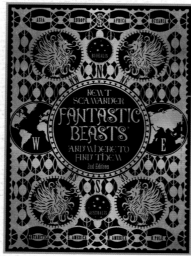

For Flourish and Blotts bookshop, the graphic designers created the cover for *A Children's Anthology of Monsters*, volume 1, and the spines for volumes 2 to 4, authored by Newt Scamander.

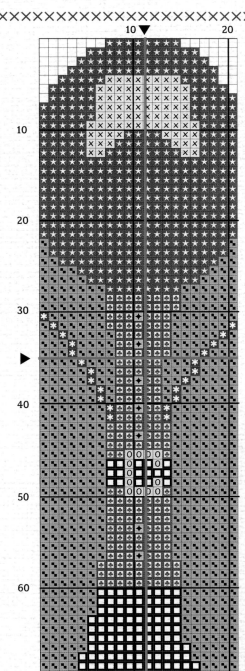

TOP TIPS:
Remember that the back will be visible for this one! To keep it as neat as possible, try running loose threads through previous stitching. And keep in mind that the blend for Hagrid's beard uses two strands of DMC 3781 and one strand of DMC 169 in the same needle.

SEVERUS SNAPE BOOKMARK

×××××××××××××××××××××××××××××

Harry unexpectedly finds himself taking Potions class in *Harry Potter and the Half-Blood Prince*. Professor Severus Snape required an "Outstanding" grade to qualify, but Harry had finished the previous year with only an "Exceeds Expectations." However, the new Potions professor this year, Horace Slughorn, is fine with that grade, so both Harry and Ron are able to attend, and are told to pick up a copy of the required textbook from the back cupboard. Of the two within, one is new, and one shabby and soiled. Ron comes up with the newer one, and Harry gets the used version. "In this case," explains graphic designer Miraphora Mina, "we had only a few seconds on-screen to show to the audience why they both want *this* book and neither of them want *that* book. They don't know *that* book has all the secrets and knowledge Harry needs for the story to evolve . . . We had to design a new version and old version that had to be quickly identifiable as the same book, but different editions."

Severus Snape wears his ubiquitous, black Edwardian-style robes for this bookmark—robes that were never redesigned but stayed the same for all eight Harry Potter films. No color substitutions allowed here!

PATTERN INFORMATION

- **FABRIC:** 14-count white perforated paper, 2 x 6 in
- **NEEDLE SIZE:** 24 tapestry needle
- **STITCH COUNT:** 21 x 70
- **FINISHED SIZE:** 1.5 x 5 in
- **MOUNTING:** N/A
- **DIFFICULTY:** Easy

	DMC FLOSS NUMBER	COLOR NAME	NUMBER OF STITICHES IN PATTERN	NUMBER OF STRANDS USED
◻	310	Black	1078	3
✕	543	Beige brown—ultra very light	87	3
Ν	775	Baby blue—very light	28	3
✳	791	Cornflower blue—very dark	43	3
★	3021	Brown gray—very dark	9	3
⊙	3841	Pale baby blue	29	3
♡	White	White	12	3

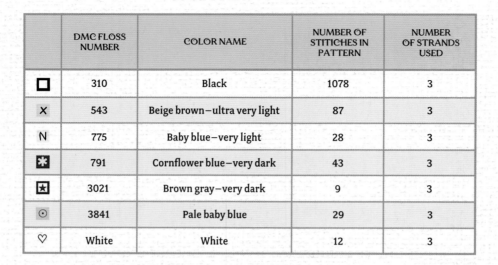

Harry's copy of *Advanced Potion-Making* was previously owned by Severus Snape—the Half-Blood Prince—in which he wrote additions or corrections to the potion instructions. Snape's handwriting was created by Miraphora Mina, who tried to imagine how Snape would write. "Probably he wouldn't have it all tidy and in the same direction," she decided, "with lots of thinking and scrubbing out."

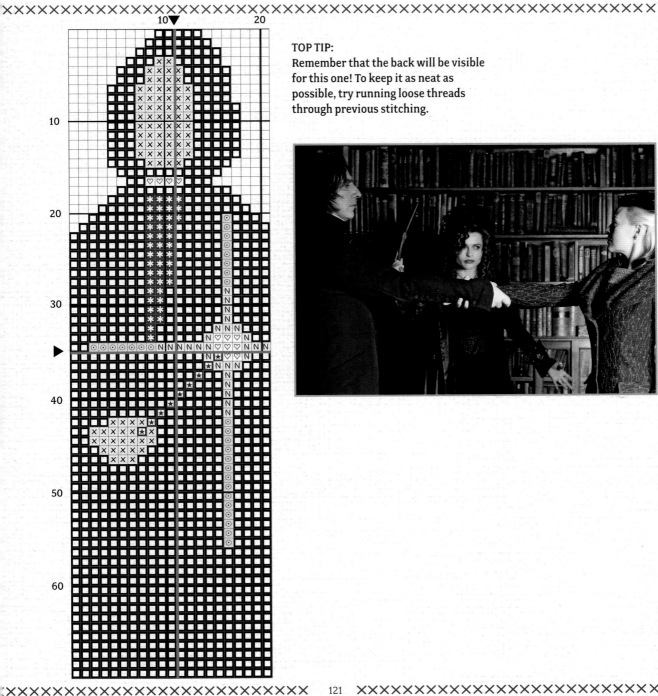

TOP TIP:
Remember that the back will be visible
for this one! To keep it as neat as
possible, try running loose threads
through previous stitching.

DUELING CLUB RUNNER BOOKMARK

In *Harry Potter and the Chamber of Secrets*, Defense Against the Dark Arts professor Gilderoy Lockhart forms a dueling club for students to learn defensive spells in a safe and practical space. The Great Hall is transformed to include a long raised platform decorated with the phases of the moon. This acts as the dueling strip for students.

Harry Potter is selected to duel Draco Malfoy—a wand battle young actors Daniel Radcliffe, playing Harry, and Tom Felton, playing Draco, enjoyed greatly. Draco first hits Harry with *Everte Statum*. For this stunt, Daniel Radcliffe wore a wire rig that flipped him up and over. Harry strikes back with the *Rictumsempra* charm. Tom Felton wore his own wire rig, which gave him more of a rolling movement when he performed the stunt. "It was a lot of fun," Felton remembers. "That was pretty exciting, doing our own stunts at thirteen or fourteen."

This dramatic bookmark has a design that can be worked in either golden yellow floss or DMC gold metallic. A bit of backstitching helps define the lines and curves as the moons wax and wane.

PATTERN INFORMATION

- **FABRIC:** 14-count navy perforated paper, 2 x 9 in
- **NEEDLE SIZE:** 24 tapestry needle
- **STITCH COUNT:** 12 x 108
- **FINISHED SIZE:** 1 x 7.75 in
- **MOUNTING:** N/A
- **DIFFICULTY:** Easy

	DMC FLOSS NUMBER	COLOR NAME	NUMBER OF STITICHES IN PATTERN	NUMBER OF STRANDS USED
●	725	Topaz	384	3
—	725	Topaz (backstitching around the moons)	33.61	1

TOP TIP:
Remember that the back will be visible for this one! To keep it as neat as possible, try running loose threads through previous stitching.

Gilderoy Lockhart has a little loop sewn on his pants to hold his wand, similar to the way a scabbard holds a sword.

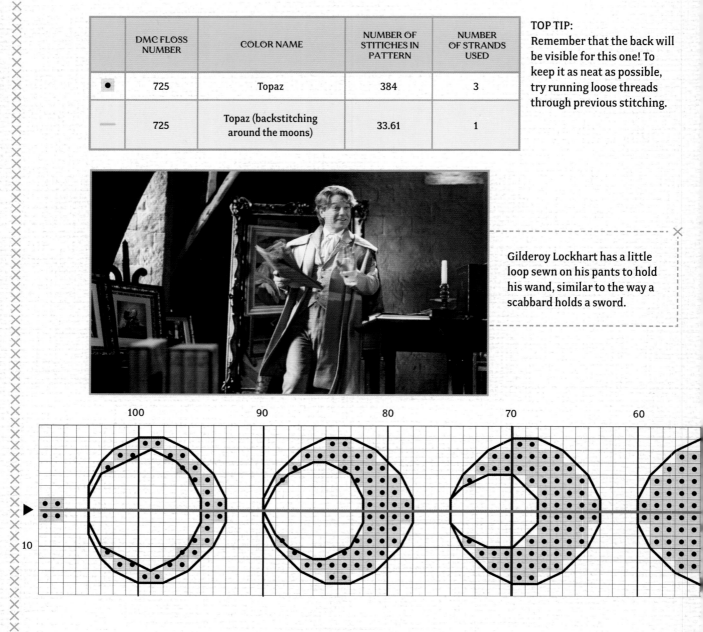

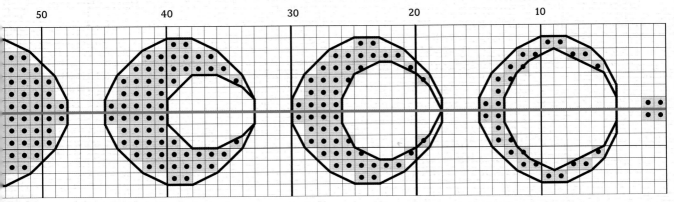

50   40   30   20   10

CHOCOLATE FROG 3-D BOX

XXXXXXXXXXXXXXXXXXXXXXXXX

Harry Potter and Ron Weasley forge a close friendship while traveling on the Hogwarts Express in *Harry Potter and the Sorcerer's Stone*, where they enjoy many selections from the Trolley Witch's cache of confectionaries. Harry is a bit reluctant, however, when he samples one of the wizarding world's favorite sweets—Chocolate Frogs—hoping they aren't *real* frogs. Ron assures him they're not, and the cards inside the box are more important anyway.

The distinctive packaging for Chocolate Frogs was created by Ruth Winick, based on a brief by production designer Stuart Craig, who drew the shape of a pentagon for her. "[He] said I should think 'classical,'" says Winick. The designer was also inspired by the Gothic architecture prevalent in Hogwarts castle's design.

The sides of this Chocolate Frog box are stitched as individual panels, then joined at the corners with an overhand stitch. One simple overlapping seam on the top creates the familiar pentagonal shape of this trinket box. Stitch the bottom half to match the top, or leave the perforated plastic exposed to allow the fragrance of potpourri, herbs, or other scented delights you can place inside to enrich your study space.

PATTERN INFORMATION

- **FABRIC:** 14-count perforated plastic, one 8 x 11 in sheet
- **NEEDLE SIZE:** 24 tapestry needle
- **STITCH COUNT (TOP):** 47 x 46
- **STITCH COUNT (EACH SIDE):** 28 x 8
- **FINISHED SIZE:** 3.5 x 3.5 x 0.1 in
- **MOUNTING:** N/A
- **DIFFICULTY:** Advanced

The graphics department labeled the Chocolate Frog as containing 70 percent of the finest *croakoa*—a mash-up of *croak* and *cacao*, aka "cocoa bean," the seed from which chocolate is made.

	DMC FLOSS NUMBER	COLOR NAME	NUMBER OF STITICHES IN PATTERN	NUMBER OF STRANDS USED
✪	9	Cocoa–very dark	52	3
◣	336	Navy blue	53	3
✳	779	Cocoa–dark	110	3
▲	782	Topaz–dark	238	3
✖	824	Blue–very dark	643	3
▣	3820	Straw–dark	1259	3
⬭	3860	Cocoa	106	3
⬤	3861	Cocoa–light	29	3
♡	Ecru	Ecru	1	3
	5282	Gold metallic pearl (whip stitching the box bottom; not on the chart)	N/A	2

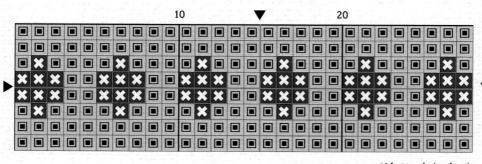

Side Panels (make 5)

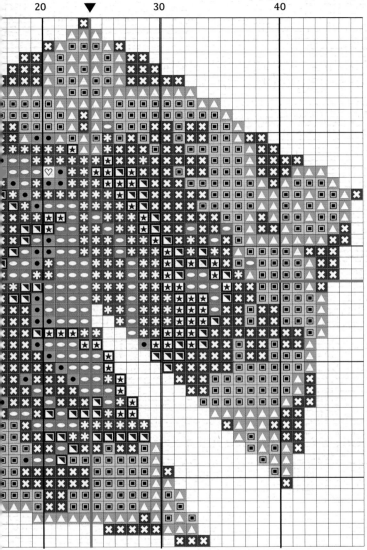

20　　　▼　　　30　　　40

Box Top

⚡ To turn this pattern into a box, stitch the top and each side panel separately. Keep the back neat by running threads through previous stitching. Then follow these steps:

1. When the embroidery is finished, carefully cut around the stitching of each piece, leaving a border of one row of the perforated plastic. Cut out the six bottom pieces and set aside.

2. To make the peak of the box lid, carefully cut the plastic along the left edge of the unstitched wedge and trim away the bottom portion of the wedge. Using the adjacent stitched areas as color references, overlap the plastic sections and cross-stitch over the seam. The holes will not line up perfectly because everything is at an angle here, so take your best stab at creating a smooth seam while stitching through both layers. You may have to wiggle the needle to find the closest hole on the underside while stitching. Be sure to cover the plastic complete at this seam; use some half stitches if you need to.

3. Attach the five side panels to the center piece with a whip stitch (see pg 28 for a reminder), using three strands each of DMC 975 and DMC 782 blended into a total of six strands together.

4. Next, connect each side panel of the box lid to its neighbor where the seams meet, using the same six strands of blended floss.

5. Make a copy of the pentagon-shape pattern for the box bottom. Use this as a guide to cut out a piece of perforated plastic measuring 1 15/16 inches on each side. Cut out five box bottom sides measuring 27 x 9 "stitches" (1 15/16 x 5/8 inches).

6. Use two strands of DMC 5282 gold metallic pearl to whip stitch the pieces of the box bottom together. If you prefer a solid gold look to the bottom, you may completely stitch all the pieces with two strands of the gold before joining the pieces to form the bottom of the box.

BERTIE BOTT'S EVERY FLAVOUR BEANS QUILL CADDY

PATTERN INFORMATION

- **FABRIC:** 14-count perforated plastic, two 8 x 11 in sheets
- **NEEDLE SIZE:** 24 tapestry needle
- **STITCH COUNT (EACH SIDE):** 34 x 73
- **FINISHED SIZE:** 2.5 x 2.5 x 5.25 in
- **MOUNTING:** N/A
- **DIFFICULTY:** Advanced

As Harry and Ron sample all sorts of sweets during their first ride together on the Hogwarts Express in *Harry Potter and the Sorcerer's Stone*, Harry is introduced to another popular wizarding treat: Bertie Bott's Every Flavour Beans. And they are *every* flavor, according to Ron: from chocolate and peppermint to spinach, liver, and tripe. When Harry hears about the possibility of consuming a bogie-flavored one, he removes the bean from his mouth and sets his container down cautiously.

The box for Bertie Bott's Every Flavour Beans was created by graphic designer Ruth Winick, who was given instructions that the packaging should be fun to open and have a "British seaside" feel.

Not only are there different flavors in Bertie Bott's Every Flavour Beans candy, but each of the four sides of the Bertie Bott's box is different, too. Stitch together the side panels at the corners, add the square bottom, and presto! You've got a place to stash your quills that will be the envy of Hogwarts.

According to *Harry Potter and the Sorcerer's Stone* director Chris Columbus, actor Rupert Grint (Ron) thought filming the scene on the Hogwarts Express "was the greatest day of his acting career, because we were just letting him eat chocolate and candy all day."

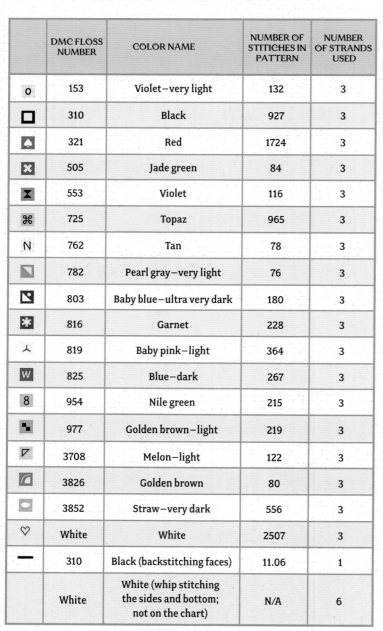

	DMC FLOSS NUMBER	COLOR NAME	NUMBER OF STITCHES IN PATTERN	NUMBER OF STRANDS USED
o	153	Violet – very light	132	3
◻	310	Black	927	3
⬟	321	Red	1724	3
✖	505	Jade green	84	3
⬛	553	Violet	116	3
⌘	725	Topaz	965	3
N	762	Tan	78	3
◣	782	Pearl gray – very light	76	3
◩	803	Baby blue – ultra very dark	180	3
✳	816	Garnet	228	3
⅄	819	Baby pink – light	364	3
W	825	Blue – dark	267	3
8	954	Nile green	215	3
◪	977	Golden brown – light	219	3
◸	3708	Melon – light	122	3
◠	3826	Golden brown	80	3
▢	3852	Straw – very dark	556	3
♡	White	White	2507	3
—	310	Black (backstitching faces)	11.06	1
	White	White (whip stitching the sides and bottom; not on the chart)	N/A	6

TOP TIPS:

⚡ **To turn this pattern into a quill caddy, follow these steps:**

1. When you finish stitching a panel, carefully cut it out, leaving one row of perforated plastic for a border. After all four sides are done, cut out a 2½-inch square of plain perforated plastic to serve as the bottom of your caddy.

2. Join the four panels along their vertical side edges with six strands of white floss, using a whip stitch. To start, knot your floss at the bottom seam of the two panels you're about to stitch together. As you whip stitch your way up, you can stitch over the knot's tail to conceal it.

3. As you work your way up each seam, occasionally tug on the panels to align them so that all four sides meet correctly at the bottom when done.

4. Once the panels are sewn together vertically, run your whip stitch across the triangular top edge of each one, again using six strands of white floss. This will create a neatly finished and consistent look.

5. Finally, use the same whip stitch one last time to attach your bottom square of plain perforated plastic to the sides of your caddy.

6. Optional: To keep quills or pens from poking through the perforations, consider cutting out a 2½-inch cardboard or cardstock square and setting it on the inside at the bottom.

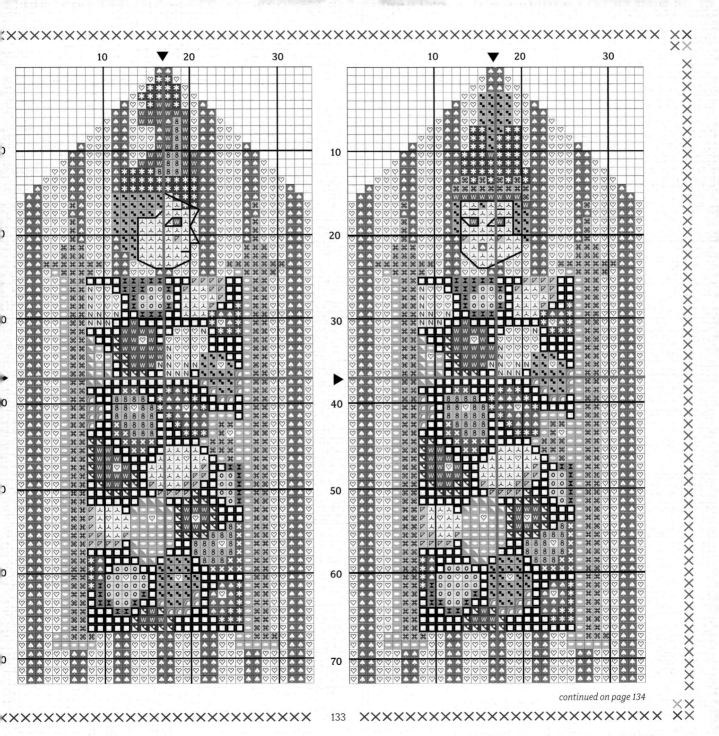

continued on page 134

continued from page 133

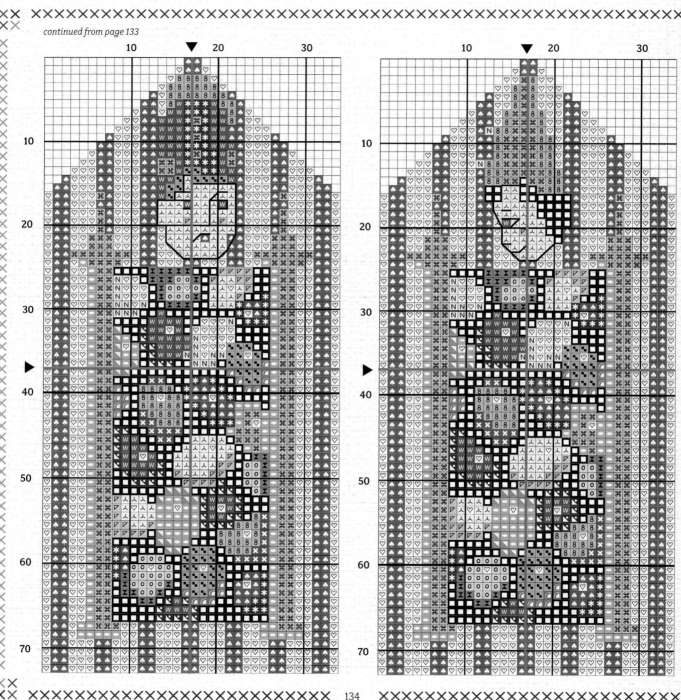

×××× ABOUT THE DESIGNER ××××

Willow Polson is an award-winning writer, artist, teacher, and filmmaker who has worked on a variety of books, magazines, films, and television shows. She is the author of several new age craft books, has been in the designer programs of DMC, Kreinik, Wichelt, Plaid, and other craft supply manufacturers. She also spent ten years as a staff designer and writer for several crafts magazines, including *Needlepoint Plus* and *Popular Woodworking*. Willow is currently in the Design Master Craftsman program with the Embroiderers' Guild of America.

×××× ABOUT THE AUTHOR ××××

Jody Revenson has written extensively about the Harry Potter films. In her first foray into the Wizarding World, she edited and contributed to the *New York Times* best sellers *Harry Potter: Film Wizardry* and *Harry Potter: Page to Screen*!

INSIGHT
EDITIONS

PO Box 3088
San Rafael, CA 94912
www.insighteditions.com

Find us on Facebook: www.facebook.com/InsightEditions
Follow us on Instagram: @insighteditions

ISBN: 979-8-88663-391-7

Publisher: Raoul Goff
VP, Group Publisher: Vanessa Lopez
VP, Creative: Chrissy Kwasnik
VP, Manufacturing: Alix Nicholaeff
Designer: Brooke McCullum
Editor: Alexis Sattler
Editorial Assistant: Jennifer Pellman
VP, Senior Executive Project Editor: Vicki Jaeger
Production Manager: Deena Hashem
Senior Production Manager, Subsidiary Rights: Lina s Palma-Temena

Pattern Designs: Willow Polson
Written by: Jody Revenson
Technical Editor: BJ Berti
Patterns Stitched: Courtney Thomas, Hannah
George, Inga Saivare, Nicole Koch, Melissa Granger,
Pat Miller, Wendy Moore, Cait Bernier, Connie
Brasher, April Mink, Karen Frank, and Willow Polson

Photoshoot Art Direction: Judy Wiatrek Trum
Photographer: Ted Thomas
Prop and Food Stylist: Elena P. Craig

ROOTS of PEACE  REPLANTED PAPER

Insight Editions, in association with Roots of Peace, will plant two trees for each tree used in the manufacturing
of this book. Roots of Peace is an internationally renowned humanitarian organization dedicated to eradicating
land mines worldwide and converting war-torn lands into productive farms and wildlife habitats. Roots of Peace
will plant two million fruit and nut trees in Afghanistan and provide farmers there with the skills and support
necessary for sustainable land use.

Manufactured in China by Insight Editions

10 9 8 7 6 5 4 3 2 1